12 STEPS TO ENLIGHTENMENT

How It Really Works

Discourses with Master Teacher

ENDEAVOR ACADEMY
Certum Est Quia Impossibile Est

12 Steps to Enlightenment:
How It Really Works
Discourses with Master Teacher

International Standard Book Number (ISBN-10): 1-890648-21-3
(ISBN-13): 978-1-890648-21-3

Library of Congress Control Number: 2013944747

Published By:
Endeavor Academy
PO Box 206
Lake Delton, WI 53940
USA

www.themasterteacher.tv
www.endeavoracademy.com
Email: publishing@endeavoracademy.com

Contents

About This Book

These are transcripts of recorded talk given extemporaneously by Master Teacher. Little or no editing has been done in the hope of maintaining and conveying the exciting, spontaneous spiritual continuity.

Master Teacher's discourses always ignite intensely emotional responses in participants as they begin to undergo their individual mental reassociation and transfiguration. You may have highly charged enthusiastic responses to this wholly dedicated, totally simple, lovingly communicated message of truth. Indeed, this outpouring of freedom to create that occurs through the release of your former necessity to retain self-inflicted loneliness, pain, aging and death, is the bright contagion of whole mind. These discourses will act as a catalyst for you, the reader, in your own self-identity of space/time, to undergo the experience of enlightenment necessary to fulfill your inevitable purpose for living: to remember you are whole and perfect as God created you.

There is a solution.

Almost none of us liked the self-searching, the leveling of pride, the confession of shortcomings which the process requires for its successful consummation. But we saw that it really worked in others, and we had come to believe in the hopelessness and futility of life as we had been living it. When, therefore, we were approached by those in whom the problem had been solved, there was nothing left to do but to pick up the simple kit of spiritual tools laid at our feet. We have found much heaven and we have been rocketed into a fourth dimension of existence of which we had not even dreamed.

The great fact is just this, and nothing less: That we have had deep and effective spiritual experiences which have revolutionized our whole attitude toward life, toward our fellows and toward God's universe. The central fact of our lives today is the absolute certainty that our Creator has entered into our hearts and lives in a way which is indeed miraculous. He has commenced to accomplish those things for us which we could never do by ourselves.

From The Big Book of Alcoholic Anonymous;
Page 25

Read it again!

A Course In Miracles and The 12-Step Program

Wherein the necessary process of awakening from your self-orchestrated dream of pain and death will be stimulated and accelerated.

These are programs of recovery from an insanely rational, self-perpetuating, objectively-temporal existence of terminal confinement that is being misconstrued as some form of the True Reality that is Eternal Life.

Peace to my mind.
Let all my thoughts be still.

Father, I come to You today to seek the peace that You alone can give. I come in silence. In the quiet of my heart, the deep recesses of my mind, I wait and listen for Your Voice. My Father, speak to me today. I come to hear Your Voice in silence and in certainty and love, sure You will hear my call and answer me.

Now do we wait in quiet. God is here, because we wait together. I am sure that He will speak to you, and you will hear. Accept my confidence, for it is yours. Our minds are joined. We wait with one intent; to hear our Father's Answer to our call, to let our thoughts be still and find His peace, to hear Him speak to us of what we are, and to reveal Himself unto His Son.

A Course In Miracles, Lesson 221

The Importance
of Anonymity in
Spiritual Awakening

Most Teachers of God in an accelerated spiritual program of mind/body enlightenment will discover in their own intense encounters with a newly-emerging reality of Christ Mind, a highly directive responsibility for personal anonymity. The more deeply-rooted this Portico of spiritual rebirth is aligned with Creative Entirety, the more persistent this guardianship will be.

An issuant union with God is sacredly unspeakable, and must be protected against the judgmental intrusion of your own corrupt self-constructed identity. Jesus speaks of this repeatedly in New Testament Gospel. And, in His *Course in Miracles*, as the necessity to guard your own Christ Child and to nurture its growth through the creative substance of continuing Holy Instants.

The early founders of the AA Program recognized with profound spiritual insight the importance of the term "anonymous." Certainly in the "confidence" of mutually-confessed "worldly unmanageability." But also in the recognition that a personal revelatory experience of the healing power of God may only be expressed through carrying a visionary message of gratitude and freedom to those still imprisoned in the inescapable cycle of drug dependence.

In this sense, everyone who discovers the reality of the "True Love of Creation" is anonymous in this world. - MT.

A Course In Miracles and the 12-Step Program

From Recovery to Enlightenment

To all recovering addicts and Course in Miracles teachers, thanks for listening. You may well be, at this moment, further along in your *homeward journey* than the "scenario of existence" you have been conjuring as "your life" in this dark continuum of fearful existence would indicate. Perhaps it's time at last to decide "enough is enough." Let's begin at the beginning and see if we can light up a cavern or two together:

The 12-Step Program is a divinely-inspired manner and method of recovery from the fatal disease of addiction to alcohol called alcoholism.

A Course In Miracles is a divinely-inspired method and manner of recovery from your addiction to a possessed conceptual self-existence, selfishly maintained by denial and rejection of the eternal love of God. It is an addiction to temporal existence and death that we will call *mortalism.*

The 12-Step Program and *A Course In Miracles* are identical. Not only are they identical in the process of the admission of a whole God or unity mind, but in the technique by which your conscious contact with God can be enhanced and, at last, fully realized.

Many of us remember the initial feeling of serenity that would come over us as we experienced the peace of mind we discovered we could share at 12-Step Meetings. A sharing of complete helplessness and surrender which, for many, brought a dramatic spiritual intervention as we turned our will and life over to the care of God. In the *Course,* it is the experience of a *Holy Instant* which is a continuing mechanism of self-realization through surrender of conceptual self-identity. For those of you who would care to examine it, the re-enactment of the *Holy Instant,* or the time of surrender, is the sole purpose of 12-Step groups and of miracle Teacher of God gatherings. The whole basis of the 12-Step Program, including the steps themselves, is to maintain a continuing conscious contact with God. This is, of course, true in the miraculous maturity of your mind to a realization of eternal wholeness that is the *Course in Miracles.*

Those of you who are coming to a 12-Step Program in the degeneration of the fact that it is completely and only a spiritual program and somehow are according it the necessity for a continuing therapeutic reassociation of the ego, are very sadly mistaken about what the 12-Step Program is. There is literally no therapy in the 12-Step Program at all except the confession of any continuing resentments you have maintained, which, as you release, become a part of the mechanism whereby you recover and discover — what? Forgiveness of yourself and those around you! This is indeed *How It Works.*

I was rummaging through my dresser this morning and have with me a copy of "*How It Works*" from the Big Book of Alcoholics Anonymous and a dog-eared, life-saving prayer book called "The Twenty-Four Hour Book" with daily prayers and instructions for an entire year. Until the time of my personal surrender I certainly had no conscious intent or even serious idea of pursuing any sort of spiritual path. Now, suddenly and miraculously, I had been given a whole new meaning and purpose for being alive.

How then did it work? Here's how. No one fails who will follow this path. All will succeed who will use the *Big Book of Alcoholics Anonymous* or the Workbook of *A Course In Miracles* to release or surrender to the certainty that there is a way out of this impossible situation. That there is a transcendent solution that brings peace and happiness. A power that is available to us right here and now. All right! This is a good beginning! Let's stay with this.

Now, the demonstration of that must be the gathering of us together in the admission that our powerlessness brought a change in our perceptual association. This is the whole basis of the *Course in Miracles* and if you will read in the Teacher's Manual, "As For The Rest," you will discover that the teaching of surrender is the whole basis for the necessity for the conscious contact with God. That's what we intend to experience right now, together, at this moment.

I discovered, as a recovered addict, following the miraculous event that occurred in my mind, that there is a mechanism of action to sustain and convey the serenity and peace of mind I had experienced. And I'm going to use the term *action* here because it's very valuable to you. The whole basis of this teaching is "today is the day" where and when, through my release of direction or misdirection of my conceptual associations, I can continually undergo an experience of — what? A spiritual awakening!

> **Step #12 — *Having had a spiritual awakening as the result of these steps, we carried this message to other associations of addictive self and practiced these principles of forgiveness in all of our affairs.***

What does this have to do with the continuing therapy or the necessity to establish a reason for our unmanageability? Nothing whatsoever. This is true to the *Course in Miracles* and to the 12-Step Program. There is no reason, ultimately, for your unmanageability. And the centering on that certainty, whether it be given to ethyl alcohol or any addictive practice, is that I have one problem and one solution. This is the core of the teaching because any problem that can be seen in the magnitude of the impossibility of the solution must be afforded a totality of solution. It's a miracle! "There's another way in which I can look at this," is exactly what *A Course In Miracles* teaches. And it teaches it as *enlightenment of mind* directly through prayer and meditation as is dictated by the 12-Step Program. The degeneration into a continuing necessity for the therapy of the possessive self-identity is exactly the causation for the continued "resedativism" of the ego as it falls back into its inherent *resentfulness*, as it's called in the 12-Step Program, or *grievance* is the word generally used in *A Course In Miracles*.

You are always meeting at a grievance of your perceptual mind. And those of you who have felt the frustration of an alcoholic mind — which all of you possess incidentally — are all part of that determination to seek justice or justification for your individual associations which, as Jesus says in the *Course*, are inherently resentful. It has nothing to do with the degree of the resentment by which you are demanding justice in your associations with yourself. *"All that I do, I do unto myself."*

What we're expressing, then, is a progression in and from the 12-Step Program to *A Course In Miracles* as an inclusion of your absolute ability, through the unconditional surrender of your addiction-to-ego, to take your place as the Savior of the World. This is very fundamental and is the natural occurrence in a determined direction, and I'm speaking here from high personal experience, that the continuing activity brings about the miracle of the release of the necessity, literally, to "participate in my dream of death." To demand recognition of myself in the correlation of my determination to assert myself and satisfy the demands that are apparent in me. I failed at that. I failed! The whole teaching of *A Course In Miracles* is to fail in your self-purpose. Are we clear on this? The whole basis of the teaching is that you cannot succeed. How abhorrent to many of you in your ego manifestations is the word "surrender." This is precisely and exactly what the 12-Step Program is. You can't get it by self-control or manageability. You must be forced into a situation of surrender or fear where you will be willing to see that there is no manner by which you can overcome your problem. And then the manifestation of the miracle will occur. It is the admission that I cannot solve the problem under any circumstance at all.

What we attempt to do in *A Course In Miracles* is to place you in a situation where you will make the admission that you are in deep fear and that the problem cannot be solved. Obviously, an alcoholic mind is aware, at a very early stage of his career of "sedativism," that he is in a great deal of fear and he cannot for the life of him, or the death of him, understand why or how associations are able to deal with the incredible slaughterhouse or purposelessness of the world in which he finds himself. In that sense, he is different. He seems to have been born in the wrong time. The *Course in Miracles* uses the term "later in time" to identify him. Do you understand? The more fearful, the later in time. The more fearful the association is, the more he has determined that the problem cannot be solved under the circumstances in which he apparently finds himself. That's a statement of fact.

So *How It Works*, then, is a continuing practice of the initial encounter where you asked for help and received it. You asked for the help of a *power greater than yourself* as a transcendent necessity, having discovered, at last, through your own futile rummaging of your mindless misappropriations of the love of God, that the problem could not be solved. This is literally the teachings of *A Course In Miracles*: the continuing practice of the experience of that instant. It's an exciting reality for the 12-Step Program people, and for those of you who are working the program of *A Course In Miracles,* to discover that, on a continuing disciplinary basis, if you work this Program, you will awaken one morning and discover that the Program is working you.

This has happened to a lot of us. And this is a practice of the discipline of getting up in the morning, and sitting quietly with the AA Twenty-Four Hour Book or the *Course* Workbook, and intentionally attempting to contact God and feeling the peace that emanates from this, and in many senses being able to deal with problems of the world which you were not heretofore able to handle, and certainly that is progress. The idea that conscious contact can continue and bring about a result that is literally miraculous each moment, and will change your life and the world you apparently inhabit, is the whole purpose of *A Course In Miracles.* Certainly it begins with some form of fundamental admission of your own unmanageability. *"Let me remember I did not make myself."*

Who can determine — or is it determinable when you walk into meetings — your readiness to really hear what the 12-Step Program teaches? Or your willingness to share, then, with these associations your mutual helplessness? All good 12-Step Program teachers understand that you come together in a meeting to share your inability to deal with the world and the recovery from addiction that you have experienced through this conscious contact with God. This is what all *Course in Miracles* groups should be. This is, indeed, what the Workbook of the *Course* is designed to bring about.

Those of you who in the past years have wondered why your 12-Step Program is resulting in your continuing, we used to call it "white knuckling," in your refusal to "Let Go and Let God," usually will admit it has directly to do with your incapacity to admit what the 12-Step Program is. The 12-Step Program is literally a surrender to God; God as you understand Him — or as we used to say, "don't understand Him." In that sense, then, the 12-Step Program is nothing but a surrender, this is the Workbook of the *Course*. And the realization that there is another way not contained within the solutions of my own conflictual mind or what is defined as my own perceptual reality. Do you see this? We discover that in our weakness is our strength. ***"Keep It Simple, Stupid."***

The simplicity of the 12-Step Program and of *A Course In Miracles* must escape the perceptual mind because it is a mechanism of self-complication. Very fundamental in the 12-Step Program is the idea of "an attitude of gratitude." It is the certainty that your sobriety or your release from the addictive captivity of drug dependence had nothing to do with your self-will but came solely from a miraculous intervention of a Higher Power. A miracle, then, is nothing but a complete momentary undoing of bondage to self-conception.

The magnitude of gratitude inherent in this miraculous occurrence of freedom is far, far beyond any conceptual explanation of it. The happy realization of *self-certainty* intrinsic in God dependency is grievously rejected and denied by the judgmental defiance of your meaningless self-will.

Rarely have we seen a person fail... How It Works. Is there anyone who goes to the meetings who really actually would sit down and read *How It Works?* How does it work? ***Rarely have we seen a person fail who has thoroughly followed our path***. It doesn't say partially or semi-thoroughly followed our path, and it doesn't say never. There was a big discussion at one of the conferences, this seems like 2000 years ago too, about why the term is "rarely" have we seen... rather than "never" have we seen a person fail... The answer to that is the same as regarding self-discovery and recovery in direct contact with the higher power of Universal Mind. Nobody can determine the method of the perseverance or dedication of the individual association. So what *rarely have we seen a* *person fail who has thoroughly followed our path* means is, who can determine what thorough is? Thorough — is it thorough surrender, or thoroughly following the path?

I can remember walking into a meeting and listening to that and entering into it without the necessity to even hear what it was saying. It's a discovery that you have found in your own mind of your indelible capacity to communicate with the universe by coming together as you are doing now. No explanation is necessary. It's a realization that true communication comes through self-discovery. That joyous self-certainty and serenity of mind are inherent in God-dependency.

Those who do not succeed are those who cannot give themselves totally to this program. There are such unfortunates. They seem to have been born that way. They are incapable of evolving a rigorous necessity for honesty, with the continual admission that I cannot solve this problem. That's being honest. "I cannot solve this problem. I don't know who I am or what in hell I'm doing here. I need help!" Now, some real spiritual progress may begin.

There are those, too, who suffer from grave emotional disorders, and we treat them as gently as we can because we understand that their emotional disorders are being brought about directly by their inability to deal with the associations of the world. We are aware of their feelings of fear and paranoia and schizophrenia, which are the direct result of their incapacity to hold themselves in the dream of fear that they are experiencing. ***They, too, can recover if they can evolve the capacity to be honest*** in realizing that it's normal for them to have experiences of fear. Attempting to overcome the fear is the antithesis of the teachings of *A Course In Miracles,* and, in fact, the 12-Step Program. It's the admission that you *cannot* overcome it. This is the only therapy that is really applicable to this teaching of a conscious contact with God. Is this so?

Our stories disclose in a general way, here we come to the 12-Step Program and here we come to *A Course In Miracles,* *what we used to be like,* and this is our continually looking at our human pursuits, isn't it? I don't want that. *What we used to be like, what happened to us,* in the discovery of the miraculous intent — ***what we used to be like, what happened, and what we are like now.*** This is a group that then comes together and says very simply, "I have had a miraculous occurrence in my own mind and I want to share the joy and happiness of the peace I have found by this experience." Isn't this so? Not studying my relationship with my mother-in-law or my ex-husband in order to hold onto the resentment of the problem I had in the first place.

So we're comparing the fundamental principles of recovery in the 12-Step Program with those of *A Course In Miracles.* We see that they begin with some admission of an absolute inability to solve the problems of your own personal existent self-identity and continue to the total necessity for a transformative spiritual experience. I saw an article in some magazine about a young recovering alcoholic who had been told by his sponsor that the 12-Step Program had nothing at all to do with *A Course In Miracles!* That the *Course in Miracles* was very complicated and mysterious and was too difficult to be understood. What nonsense! We're very determined here that you understand the fundamental basis of both of these teachings. Don't get caught in the wash of therapy. These are programs of continuing conscious contact with God or Universal Mind that free you from the insanity of an intolerable, worldly self-conception that required an ever-increasing "sedativism." ***"I am free from self-will run riot."***

Can you come and teach with me our certainty of having had the experience of the miracle of sobriety and the continuing miracle of self-realization that is this direct method of communication with Eternal Reality?

How inevitable the consciousness of Bill Wilson, one of the founders of AA, who was a typically helpless example of total addiction to "any relief" from the impossible situation of this world, who finally underwent the horrendous experience of a dark night of the soul — a "Father, why hast thou forsaken me?" to a "Father into Thy hands I commend my spirit" advent of a phenomenal, physically-illuminatory experience of transformation. Bill's bed at the hospital, as witnessed by several nurses in his room, was literally *enveloped in light.* Where will you personally deal with an inexplicable transfiguration of this nature? It is impossible to say. The only possible measurement is totally present in your own personal dilemma expressed as the frustration and futility that occurs in your own need to find a true meaning and purpose for your existence in this world. Be assured of this: the entire reclamation project of the 12-Step Program and *A Course In Miracles* is totally based on a divine revealing of, and intervention by, our very own individual and universal source of reality, which is the eternally-creating mind of God.

It is important to remember that the programs are not a perceptual admission of the necessity for some sort of bottoming out. They are the natural, inevitable result of the surrender itself. They are both the cause and the effect. Can you hear this? In any prayer, the cause and the effect are actually simultaneous. The teaching of the *Course* is you literally cannot get more than you are asking for, but you will indeed get what you are asking for. Do you see this? So that the broader your range of surrender, the more mentally and emotionally edifying will be the simultaneously-corrective response of the Holy Spirit. There is nothing to deny your own intentions because nothing is outside of you. If you ask for the peace of God, and truly desire it, you will have the peace of God because the peace of God is what you are.

So the first time that you hear this message, and the second time, and the tenth, and the twentieth time, and the hundredth time, and *How It Works* at meetings, or *How It Works* in *A Course In Miracles* groups, will dictate the terms under which you are absolutely, unqualifyingly willing to accept that you have a very serious authority problem in regard to the making of yourself and the necessity and determination to die. And the relief that you feel when you come into a group of this nature is not expressible, but those of you who have been to what we would term "good" meetings where there is no therapy, just a mutual recognition, can sense the feeling of a high camaraderie through the admission of the powerlessness of that identity or association and it is very, very noticeable. Your concern is not therapy at all.

I'll speak as a Program member for a moment here: If you've got a beginner who is going to give you what we call a "drunk-a-log," he is determined to tell the story of the circumstances that indicated how completely powerless he was. Certainly these are necessary and important admissions. Much as if you came into a *Course* group and said, "I just can't deal with this world. Everything I do is futile." This is simply an admission of qualification for membership. Any counseling advice should not occur. The member has one problem and has been given the solution. In no regard would any recovering addict take the inventory of the other person. Do you understand? I'm not going to take the inventory of that association. I have enough problems in my dedication to my own recovery. The therapy that I would offer him would only be based on my determination not to have an experience myself, but rather to verify his resentments in association with himself rather than admitting that we really only had one problem and that problem is the drug itself.

All Program meetings and all *Course in Miracles* groups say that you have one problem. You may call it alcohol, you may call it ego, you can call it self-perception, you can call it determination to affront God — I'm not concerned with what you call it. All of it is a limited self-identity or an addiction to the necessity of the assertion of your limited consciousness-mind. Does that make any sense? So here we come together in a sensible purpose of undergoing the miracle or the experience in our dedication to the certainty that the problem is not solvable. ***Don't analyze. Utilize.***

Here's *How It Works.* ***There are those, too, who suffer from grave emotional and mental disorders, but many of them do recover if they have the capacity to be honest.*** Here it is. ***Our stories disclose in a general way what we used to be like, what happened, and what we are like now.*** If you have decided, individually, in your own mind, that you want what we have, never mind that you are able to discern it by your own mechanisms. The decision is that you are willing to become Teachers of God and declare an association of yourself that is giving you joy and happiness. You're looking at other associations who are ready to give up their inventory of total death and sickness, and are asking, as when you came to the Program, "How did you get this?" "How did you come to know this?" This is the mechanism you're teaching as the 12-Step Program and *A Course In Miracles.*

First of all you have to want it, don't you? You have to be able to see the difference between the pain that you are in and the apparent joy that this association is experiencing. And the first thing he will tell you in his genuine association is — what? He didn't have anything to do with it! Do you see? All good programs will teach, "I had nothing to do with it. I gave up, and I had the miraculous experience of the non-need to continue to sedate myself. It was a miracle." I want the mechanism, which is the 12-Step Program, of continuing to have that experience. I want to have it all the time.

Now, if you decide that you want what we have and are willing to go to some *lengths to get it...* Oh, it doesn't say *some* lengths. No, no! It doesn't say compromise! It says, *"are willing to go to any lengths to get it."* Now, obviously the guy who is going to continue, if you really taught this, who is going to continue to demand attention to his addiction, will say, "I'm not willing to go to *any* lengths. I can still solve my problem." This is the basis of the teaching. But ***if you're***

willing to go to any lengths, you're ready to take certain steps. You're ready to make particular applications of the necessity for the miracle in the Workbook. These are steps aren't they? In the Workbook? Now, some of them we are going to refuse to do. Some of them will be easier for you to do than others because you have a tenacity to continue to verify the necessity to exist in time and die. And that's very inherent in you. All of your human memories verify your addiction to self-possessive termination.

And, at some of these steps you're going to balk. Why? ***You still think you can find an easier and softer way to the solution.*** It's a lot easier for me not to have to listen to you, Jesus of Nazareth. It's a lot easier for me not to have to listen to the inevitability of my surrender in order to have the experience. I would rather assert a compromise to Your direction that "Thy will be done on earth as it is in Heaven" so I can continue to direct my own program. Any good, and I'm using the term "recovered," alcoholic knows perfectly well that the more he directs his associations, the more resentment he will retain in the necessity for the expression of himself. That's a fact. ***"Let Go and Let God." "Get Out of the Driver's Seat." "Go the Extra Mile." "But for the Grace of God..."*** What's ever happened to all these expressions? They're too spiritual. They are ultimately nothing but a confession of God-need.

We thought we could find an easier, softer way, but what? ***We couldn't.*** Notice that this is past tense. The 12-Step Program is the admission that you have evolved and are in Heaven. Even the Twelfth Step says having had a spiritual awakening, we continue to do it, but our problem has been solved by our continual contact. There's no necessity to indicate another solution. Our certainty that the problem cannot be solved is the continuing admission of this contact with God. ***Today I will judge nothing that occurs.***

But we couldn't. Now, ***with all the earnestness at our command***, all of it, with everything that we can tell you as a mind who came to know this, that we can possibly give you, *we beg of you to be fearless and thorough from the very start*. Look at all of this conceptual world as not being able to be understood. Say immediately, everything here is only totally chaotic. *Be fearless and thorough from the very start.* Why is this necessary? *Some of us have tried to hold onto our old ideas and the result was nil until we let go absolutely.* That is a direct statement from *A Course In Miracles*. You think you're getting a result from your own retention of resentment but the result is actually nil. You are getting no result at all except the continuing fear within your own mind. *The result was nil until,* you're not going to like this sentence, *until we let go absolutely.* Is that all right?

Remember that you're dealing with an ego/alcoholic/self-identity. You're dealing with the necessity to sedate yourself, to give yourself credit for your associations, to justify the resentment and fear that you feel in your own mind. Jesus would say of the ego: it's *cunning*, it's *baffling*, and it's *powerful*, and *without help, it's way too much for you to ever do.* You need the Holy Spirit to bring you to the attention that you cannot solve the problem. *But there is One who has all power — that One is God. May you find Him now!* That's a high prayer. May you find Him. It's a request that you find Him through your determination not to solve this. *May you find Him now! Remember, He isn't lost, you are!*

Half measures availed us nothing. Half measures avail you nothing. A compromise of your determination to correlate the sickness, pain, death and loneliness of earth with eternal love and joy and happiness of Heaven will not work. *Half measures availed us nothing.* A full measure is what God is. A half measure is what separation is. It will avail you nothing. You cannot avail of your own death wish and expect to solve the problem.

Where did you stand? *At the turning point*. When Jesus teaches this in the *Course*, again and again and again, He will say, you're at a turning point now. Are you able to see that this is a turning point? Will you allow your mind to come into this point that you have always come to before, and then, determine to see a result in half measure, rather than — what? As this sentence says, **we asked His protection and care with complete abandon**. This is the core of the teachings of *A Course In Miracles*.

My joy and happiness, guys, those of you who want to hear this, you can make this academic if you want to, you can study all the reasons and the reassociations you want to; the fact of the matter is that my peace and joy are my complete dependence on God or a higher power, a certainty that of and by myself I am nothing. It has nothing to do with what I am dependent on. What is that? That's *complete abandon*. Notice that the joy is in the abandon. You can direct it to God but only if you understand Him anyway. Abandonment in that sense is giving, isn't it? I'm going to abandon my need. I'm going to only give. I will not be possessed by the necessity to hold on and to retain. I will abandon that and I will say, "Father into Thy hands I commend my spirit."

Here are the steps we took. Past tense — it worked didn't it? — a day at a time. As a program of recovery we admitted what? **Step #1 — We were absolutely powerless over everything and our life was unmanageable**. We are powerless. I don't care what it's over. I can't solve this problem. You know in your hearts you can't solve this problem, and you've covered it up. I don't care how much joy you're getting out of the certainty that you can. Fundamentally, you know that you can't solve the problem or you wouldn't be seeking happiness. You are seeking happiness with the admission that you can solve the problem, but you can't. The problem is not solvable in that sense.

Step #2 — We came to believe, through the futility of our own expressions, **that a Power greater than ourselves could restore us to sanity**. What a lovely use of the word sanity and insanity. The *Course* teaches you directly that you are insane and that all of your efforts in regard to this don't require a definition of what insanity is. I've known a lot of alkies in my day who admit they acted very insanely when they drove a car or did all the crazy things that they do in their continuing unmanageability. The admission that the whole association is insane and that the manner in which they could be restored to sanity transcended their capacity is the second step of the Program, which goes to the third, which is literally the Workbook of the *Course*:

Step #3 — *Made a decision to turn our will and our lives over to the care of God as we understand Him.* I'm going to turn it over. I'm not able to solve the problem. Is that okay? "That's very weak. Isn't that an admission of your powerlessness?" Yes! Yes, those of you who are determined to assert yourself, can do that, but you will then continue to — what? Assume the guilt for the necessity of your self-identity and you're going to take on that burden of guilt. It's going to give you a sense of resentment because you're going to demand justice within this association, aren't you?

What do you do after you've done all that? Step #3 — You've done this and it's working. You've turned your will and your life over to the care of God and you're having — this is the Workbook now — you're having all of these lovely experiences and your whole life is changing. But now, there's some necessary things to do. This is the Workbook, along with the rest of the Steps of the Program.

Step #4 — *We made a searching and fearless moral inventory of ourselves.* Now, if you want to get caught up in what "moral" means, go ahead. Remember that the emphasis is on *fearless*. You cannot be forgiven until you make a fundamental admission of your guilt. You can go out and teach all you want, "I'm not guilty," and, "I'm forgiven." The direction is that you are in a condition of the guilt of self-inflicted pain, and that it's perfectly proper for you to take an inventory of the associations in which you find yourself. Notice that it doesn't say that the inventory must always be degrading. They will allow you to have all the pride you want in your necessity to compare yourself with what you consider to be the injustices around you. But remember, the relinquishment of your resentments against yourself and your surroundings (in the *Course,* Jesus calls them grievances) is absolutely necessary in order to experience the peace of God.

Look to this day, for it is life, the very life of life.

Now, if you're going to do **Step #5**, the requirement is that you admit or undergo an atonement in your incapacity to deal with the sin in which you find yourself. This is actually an on-going process in the miracle. Who do you have to admit to? ***You admit to God, to yourself, and to another human being the exact nature of your wrong doing.*** Is it necessary for you to? Admitting to God is pretty easy; admitting to yourself is pretty easy; admitting to another human being requires the necessity for you to forgive yourself in your relationship with him and it can be very valuable to you. So this is an admission of our capacity to share a union or a new identity based on the surrender of our self-will. We are becoming ready to accept forgiveness of ourselves and those around us. ***Today, well lived, makes every yesterday a dream of happiness and every tomorrow a vision of hope.***

The Sixth Step is a particular step that is taught in *A Course In Miracles* as a continuing examination of your association. ***We're entirely ready to have God remove all these defects of character.*** In our associations with Bill Wilson, we talked about whether you can ever be entirely ready to do anything. But remember, there is a determination here that you have turned your will and your life over to the care of God. So that, while you cannot determine your readiness, you can stay vigilant in your dedication that the miracle is working in your own mind. This is greatly emphasized in the Workbook of the *Course*. Stay single-minded and you cannot fail.

Step #7 — *Humbly ask Him to remove our shortcomings.*
Father, help me to see myself as you see me. I have fallen
short of the goal of perfect love and happiness you set for me.
Don't let my resentment of my own shortfall blind me to the
light of this new life.

Now you're going to what? **Step #8 —** *Make a list of all the*
persons you harmed, and became willing to make amends to
them all. First it says you don't make the amend immediately;
you evolve a willingness to do so. That's a very interesting
idea. That the willingness comes before the action itself. Not
that it can be measured, but somewhere there's a discipline
involved in your willingness to admit to the people you have
harmed, through your old dedication to remain in your own
selfish, possessive association with yourself, that you have
discovered through a spiritual experience a new you! That a
miracle has happened and is happening!

Then what? **Step #9 —** Then you *make direct amends,* literally,
to such persons wherever possible, except when to do so
would injure them or others. I want to say this to you, and I
want you to hear this and this goes for 12-Step Programmers
as well as Miraclists: The result of the amend that you are
willing to make has nothing at all to do with the amend itself.
The purgation that occurs at your capacity to confess or ask
for forgiveness is the necessity. In truth, whether your amend
is accepted or rejected matters not. Many of you are very
fearful of the result you're going to get by asking for total
forgiveness. In the *Course,* Jesus teaches this: that the ego
is going to be affronted by you. No matter how much you
demand that it forgive you, it is not going to forgive you in
that association, and you are looking for a limited result of
the purgation of your own mind, that is, a necessity for you
to justify the forgiveness in the first place. And to the direct
extent you look for a *quid pro quo* or an exchange of the
mutualness of your guilt, you will not do a satisfactory step.
The cleansing is always individual through the forgiveness or

the recognition that you are as God created you. And there is, literally, no reciprocity involved in it. I know to some of you that may seem selfish because you're going to continue to demand a necessity to justify the evil that you think you did in order that you can continue to share it. That is not what this says and it's not finally what you must do. Remember you must be and are always only perfect as God created you.

Now to **Step #10 — *Continued to take personal inventory and when we were wrong promptly admitted it.*** This is a crucial part of the 12-Step Program and also of the *Course in Miracles* program. Your ability to stay in a continual condition of confession where you don't lay up the stores of resentment that have held you in your situation or bondage to the grievance are important keys to the teachings both of the 12-Step and Miracles Program. ***"Easy Does It Now..." "I'm doing this to myself."***

Perhaps now you think that the application of Step #10 is not so important. Perhaps you've fallen into all sorts of philosophies and perceptions about what the *Course in Miracles* is. Listen: *A Course In Miracles* is nothing but a psychology of total forgiveness and the value of taking an inventory at night before you go to bed, about seeking not to have harmed anybody, and making that amend immediately, and that will keep you on the track to salvation. And I'm speaking from deep experience in this, because working the Program, or the discipline of running an inventory in your mind at the end of the day so that you don't carry over the possession of the grievance, is crucial. Why? If you carry it, you will justify it in the resentment of the association of your old, meaningless conceptual mind. Don't let the sun set on a grievance, because if you can only do it now, the necessity to hold onto the resentment justifies the past action and holds you in the bondage of your old association. Cause no one pain. Wow! Talk about a day at a time! Or as the *Course* teaches — an hour or a minute or a *Holy Instant!*

You look at the condition of the resentment of the world in its determination to continue to punish and justify an old association and you can see exactly what you need to look at in your own mind. And to live a life in order to justify that somebody be continually punished, or held in prison or killed is just a waste of your life. What a terrible waste it is to watch these television programs where there's a confrontation that "you did this to me twenty years ago and I'm going to hold onto that until the day I die." That's a wasted life, guys. What a useless, meaningless condition of existence. You listen to me. I'm going to offer you a little therapy. I'm not at all concerned about how you hear this. I'm telling you that any grievance is simply bondage to pain, loneliness and death. Any association, in its demand for vengeance, is inflicting pain on itself and that "self." What is the difference between a prisoner and a guard? Nothing. Both are condemned to that association of the grievance. See that? What a terrible thing to go through life as what the perceptual mind is, a constant need to get even; to punish these other associations, which are really nothing but your determination to hold onto your grievance, and to suffer pain and death.

So you continue to take a personal inventory and when you're wrong, promptly admit it. This is exactly the same teaching as don't lay up stores. But it's very difficult for you to see. Every possession that you hold onto binds you to the retrospect of the necessity to justify the death that you're proceeding to. Do you see how this is?

Each day this whole teaching, and the manner in which many of you initially obtained sobriety or the direction of turning your will over to the care of God, came about by the admission of "*today is today.* I will not be concerned about yesterday or last week; those things are gone, and there's nothing I can do about that but ask for release from them." They cannot be changed because they're already gone. How deep is the resentment of an alcoholic mind, or a perceptual mind, who is determined to base his reality on a resentment or a miscalculation or a mistake or what he calls a sin that happened to him twenty years ago; ten, twenty, thirty, forty, fifty years ago? And the inevitability of the frustration he feels by his inability to change it, and he is condemned, then, to suffer the result of that. Why? He has sequenced time in his own mind and he is determined to base his reality on that previous experience. All previous experiences are only grievances. And this is the first thing my sponsor told me on the Program. Don't ask for justice, ask for mercy. When I first came to meetings, I began to say things like, "Well I know, but I had..." He said, "Stop it! Ask for mercy, dummy."

The teaching is "you're on borrowed time" anyway. The whole teaching is that you've borrowed just a moment from eternity. Can you hear this? Now that you've got this chance, call it a *Holy Instant* and use it to recognize your return to Heaven. You see that there is a way that you can live rather than die. You borrowed eternity and put a moment of it into time. That's a lovely idea, isn't it? This is the same idea as the conversion and enlightenment of your mind. It's the same idea as having a death experience where you understand that you're alive by a grace that transcends your self-identity, and this will make you very happy. You're in grace. What? You've commended your spirit to God. That's the whole idea. That's personal inventory, isn't it? That's your own deep dark secrets about yourself — the one you blame your neighbor for. The heck with that! Let go and let God! Each one of you retains one particular special grievance. Do you know that? Would you care to look at that one? I have one. It's the whole world. And I assumed responsibility for my determination to help lead you out of this hell.

Miracles teachers see immediately that **Step #11** is a description of the entire program of transformation that is the Workbook of the *Course in Miracles*. Listen! ***Sought through prayer and meditation to continually improve our conscious***

contact with God as we didn't understand Him... Whoops! **...as we understand Him, praying only for knowledge of His will for us and the power to carry it** through the spirit.

And then the very beautiful last step, **#12: *Having had a spiritual awakening as a result of these steps*** — notice this is past tense. It's happening to you! First you work it, then it works you. First you apply the discipline of the Workbook, then you discover that the Workbook is real. It really works! Once you discover that the miracle of God contact is real, the discipline becomes simple. And finally, there's no discipline at all because the natural occurrence of the joy is the turning of your will and your life over to God. ***Having had a spiritual awakening as the result of these steps, we tried to carry this message to alcoholics.*** We tried to carry it to other human sufferers — to other "mortalholics."

This is you as a teacher of God, isn't it? This is you as the Savior of the World. ***And to practice these principles in all of our affairs.*** That is all you're asked to do. The discipline is to stay in this constant necessity for the reassociation of your mind with the admission that the miracle is always working all about you if you'll let it. Can you see this? It's always happening to you. Step back — feel the indescribable happiness of your true reality! The resistance is always in your own perceptual mind. We can't tell you what love and God is, but we can tell you what the obstacle to love is. This is the determination of yourself to hold yourself in this bondage of ego, in this bondage of the addiction to the necessity for your self-identity.

"Wow," some of us said. "I'm not going to go through with that. What an order!" ***What an order! I can't go through with it.*** And many of the associations that will come in contact with the teachings of *A Course In Miracles* will say, "What an order! I can't go through with it." ***Do not be discouraged. No one among us has been able to maintain anything like perfect adherence to these principles.*** Why? There is no definition of perfection. I'm not teaching you to an establishment of the manner by which I accomplished this. I'm telling you it's a continual reassociation of your own mind. You're the one that is seeking for the result. I'm not offering you result. There's no manner by which you can do this. The admission of our powerlessness, our helplessness, is what salvation is. And this is actually what this says: **We are not saints. The point is we are willing to grow along spiritual lines.** In that sense, we are claiming only momentary spiritual progress to this determination because the result is not here. But we open our hearts and our minds. We have the experience of the miracle of the loss of the conflict of our perceptual identity and we enter into a union with God which is the basis of all of the teachings. **"God is the Mind with which I think." "Thy Will not my will be done."**

Here's our **description of the human, and there's a chapter to the agnostic** (those of you who believe that the *Course in Miracles* is written in the vernacular of Christianity, and tend therefore to reject it, for example), **and your personal adventures, which are a part of your own mind before and after, make three things very clear**: That we were unmanageable, **that we were alcoholic;** that we were in our own perceptual self and that **we could not manage our own lives** no matter what we did; and that **no human power could have relieved our alcoholism** or our fearful human condition because we were locked in the disease of mortalism. But **that God could and would if He were sought**. It doesn't say "found." Does it? It says, *"sought."* It doesn't say God could and would if He were found. God isn't lost. The act of seeking God is what the peace of God is. The act of the release is what the peace is. "Thank You." That's a prayer, isn't it? **"My Father gives all power unto me."**

So is this a prayer meeting that we're having? Is this a communion with God? Have you made an agreement among yourselves not to discuss your own personal grievances because they're meaningless? Somewhere. Somewhere you have undergone a transition where you have no intention of bringing your individual grievances or self-identity into this attempt at union with God. This is the admission of a conversion, a freedom from the bondage of this world of death. A meeting of Mortalholics Anonymous! This is the whole basis and only purpose of *A Course In Miracles*. I'm not going to bring my grievance into the meeting and justify the grievance. I'm going to come to an AA meeting, I'm going to come to a *Course* group, and simply acknowledge that I am perfect as God created me. And through the release of the necessity to hold the grievance, I will have the experience of the joy and happiness of God. ***"I am the Light of the world."***

How exciting that, at last, this world has a purpose: to teach and learn together the unlimited power of the whole universe that is ours through the creative love of God — the revelation that you are experiencing in the release of your own conceptual self-identity. The core of the curriculum is that you are no longer feeling responsible for the sickness and pain and death that is inherent in the human mind; and that you are, in fact, undergoing this enlightenment or experience or miracle of the turning of your self-will over to the will of God. All right. And it's the act of doing it, that is what the miracle is. And it is continuous and it is going on all the time. What an incredible discovery! The Workbook of *A Course In Miracles* is nothing but a practice in prayer. It is a catechism on how to pray, only because you need the discipline of how to pray. This is a prayer session and we'll do a couple of prayers for you.

Feel the magnificently divine truth of these prayers as directed to you by the resurrected mind of Jesus Christ:

> *How foolish, Father, to believe Your Son could cause himself to suffer! Could he make a plan for his damnation, and be left without a certain way to his release? You love me, Father. You could never*

leave me desolate, to die within a world of pain and cruelty. How could I ever think that Love has left Itself? There is no will except the Will of Love. Fear is a dream, and has no will that can conflict with Yours. Conflict is sleep, and peace awakening. Death is illusion; life, eternal truth. There is no opposition to Your Will. There is no conflict, for my will is Yours.

Forgiveness shows us that God's Will is one, and that we share it. Let us look upon the holy sights forgiveness shows today, that we may find the peace of God. Amen. (Lesson 331)

I will not wait another day to find the treasures that my Father offers me. Illusions are all vain, and dreams are gone even while they are woven out of thoughts that rest on false perceptions. Let me not accept such meager gifts again today. God's voice is offering the peace of God to all who hear and choose to follow Him. This is my choice today. This is my choice. *And so I go to find the treasures God has given me.* I'm not going to participate, I'm going to lay down this burden of self and I'm going to find the treasure of my own awakening. *I seek but the eternal. For Your Son can be content with nothing less than this. What, then, can be his solace but what You are offering to his bewildered mind and frightened heart, to give him certainty and bring him peace? Today I would behold my brother sinless. This Your Will for me, for so will I behold my own sinlessness. (Lesson 334)*

Listen! Here's everything you ever need to know about your recovery from the meaningless journey into fear that is your perceptual self-identity:

I've come to know that *I am affected only by my own thoughts* and I am determined that I am a thought only of You as You have created me. *It needs but this to let*

25

salvation come to all the world because I have created all the world in my fearful thoughts, but I am being affected only by my own thoughts. *For in this single thought is everyone released at last from fear.* I intend to release my brother from the judgment I have laid on him in order to keep my own identity. I'm not going to hold a resentment in my mind in order to justify our relationships. *Now has he learned that no one frightens him, and nothing can endanger him.* I have no enemies, and I am safe from all external things. My thoughts can frighten me, but since these thoughts belong to me alone, I have the power to change them and exchange each fear thought for a happy thought of love. I am crucifying myself. I'm not going to do it anymore. God has a plan that His beloved Son will be redeemed and was redeemed.

Your plan is sure, my Father, — only Yours. All other plans will fail. And I will have thoughts that will frighten me, until I learn that You have given me the only Thought that leads me to salvation. Mine alone will fail, and lead me nowhere. Just my own, just my own idea. *But the Thought You gave me promises to lead me home, because it holds Your promise to Your Son. (Lesson 338)*

These are the prayer lessons of the Workbook of *A Course In Miracles*. Our meeting together today was an attempt to get you to enter into the experience of the release of the necessity to continue with your addiction to pain and death and time. And this under the auspices of the direction of your own mind through the 12-Step Program which came from a miraculous intervention. And your life-saving *Course in Miracles* Program that is resurrected mind awakening you from your own nightmare. You, individually, in your own dream of death and pain can undergo the experience of the miracle. The steps to awakening from your dream of death begin with the admission and recognition of your incapacity to deal with this and the discovery that there is another way to live that is not constituted in your perception as you identify yourself. Literally, an expansion of your own mind. To what? A communion and a union with the power of the Universe which is what you are.

Heavenly Father, we thank You that this has come about in us and we are certain now of the glory of the revelation of these steps and of this Program. And we are happy that we have found ourselves in this late sojourn of mind among those willing to make the confession of pain and death and the need not to be found guilty in their own self-identity with the admission that God only forgives because God is what your Universal Mind is. In this, we remain thankful. And in this, we abide. And in this, our truth is, forever and ever. Amen.

I want you to understand that when I am speaking of this, I am speaking directly from my own personal experience of surrender that founded my program of sobriety and serenity and of a continuing need to carry this message that fostered my passage to enlightenment. It is very possible for you in an awakening mind to rummage through what brought you to this. And if that's an expression of continual gratitude, the total power of God's love will be yours as you give it away. If it's an expression of the necessity to reassociate, to demand the attention to what you think are the needs of your self-containment, of your own determination to sustain yourself, you're going to remain in the temporal order of the futile existence of mortalism. Isn't this so? That's a statement of fact. How very simple it finally is!

I can only give to myself.

If I defend myself I'll be attacked.

You are causing your own grievance and you are not going to do it anymore. It's amazing how far the 12-Step Program or what you call *A Course In Miracles* programs can get off the track in regard to what it offers and guarantees. And the reason is that it is both difficult and simple at the same time. They both declare literally that peace and joy come from a renunciation of your own self-conceived associations. There's no other way that this can occur. It requires the experience of sharing the joy of the certainty of the confession of your helplessness, and the experience of a whole new reality, not of temporal existence, but a part of Eternal Life.

Having shared an incredible need for justification of life on this earth, I understand the calamity of the word surrender. While I was perfectly willing to finally admit that I had suffered from a powerlessness and that a continuing recovery from my addiction was occurring, the idea of the total surrender, which was the continuing mechanism of my enlightenment, was difficult for me. What many will discover, as I did, was that my necessity to carry the message in the twelfth step practice allowed me to observe the miracle of sudden recovery in action.

What happened was, and what happens with many of you, your revelatory reassociation causes you to recognize the 12-Step Program as a healing mechanism in which you immediately enter. The same thing will happen with many consciousnesses who have had revelatory reassociations in broad ranges of self when they pick up *A Course In Miracles.* They will immediately be able to see it or discern it at that level of the recognition of their own mind. This, then, is just a practice of a continuing new visionary experience of re-identification of yourself within your own mind. But the value is never in the mechanism or method. The value is only in the continuing grace of this newly-discovered reality.

You're where you belong at last. When you discover a group that is in full admission of the sharing of an experience of recovery, you will feel virtually immediately the release of your own necessity to protect and justify the fearful possession of your own resentments. You have come together to share the miracle of a complete healing from a fatal disease of mind and body. The serene certainty of your recovery is privately acknowledged and protected through honoring your individual anonymity. You are in this world, but not of it.

And that's literally a communicative experience. You don't limit yourself to the old impossible you. You have made the fundamental admission that you have gathered for the purpose of sobriety rather than to determine by judgment the value that you have in your own identity of yourself. Quite literally, "I can't solve this problem." "I can't either." "It's not solvable." "I know it." "How are you getting along?" "Fine, as long as I don't." Not: "How well are you dealing with it?" Rather: "How well are you *not* dealing with it?" *"I can't, He will if I let Him."*

The admission in both teachings is that the resentment can be released immediately because you *are* the resentment. And the *Holy Instant* is inevitably the moment that you release it because your addiction to your own self-willed existence is what the grievance was. Now are you whole and alive in the fullest measure as the miracle of God-dependence frees you from the bondage of self-inflicted pain, loneliness and death of this world. And now a joyous reunion of our minds occurs.

The sharing of the experience of the miracle is an imperative part of our awakening to the reality of Eternal Life. We offer to each other and the world our vision of a completely new meaning and purpose for this apparent aggregation in time and space.

That I was present at your miracle happening had to do with the certainty that I could share with you my miraculous experience of healing, not as identified in the situation of the world. In the sharing of the healing grace of the love and light of God, our minds communicate the simple and incredibly exciting realization that we are whole and perfect and eternally alive as God created us.

This indeed is the entire healing process of the illumination of your mind through the process of *A Course In Miracles*:

The roads this world can offer seem to be quite large in number, but the time must come when everyone begins to see how like they are to one another. Men have died on seeing this, because they saw no way except the pathways offered by the world. And learning they led nowhere, lost their hope. And yet this was the time when they could have learned their greatest lesson. All must reach this point, and go beyond it.

————◆◆×◆◆————

It seems to you the world will utterly abandon you if you but raise your eyes. Yet all that will occur is you will leave the world forever. This is the re-establishment of your will. Look upon it, open-eyed, and you will nevermore believe that you are at the mercy of things beyond you, forces you cannot control, and thoughts that come to you against your will. It is your will to look on this. No mad desire, no trivial impulse to forget again, no stab of fear nor the cold sweat of seeming death can stand against your will. For what attracts you from beyond the veil is also deep within you, unseparated from it and completely one.

Each day, and every minute in each day, and every instant that each minute holds, you but relive the single instant when the time of terror took the place of love. And so you die each day to live again, until you cross the gap between the past and present, which is not a gap at all. Such is each life; a seeming interval from birth to death and on to life again, a repetition of an instant gone by long ago that cannot be relived. And all of time is but the mad belief that what is over is still here and now. Forgive the past and let it go, for it is gone. You stand no longer on the ground that lies between the worlds. You have gone on, and reached the world that lies at Heaven's gate. There is no hindrance to the Will of God, nor any need that you repeat again a journey that was over long ago.

Not one light in Heaven but goes with you. Not one Ray that shines forever in the Mind of God but shines on you. Heaven is joined with you in your advance to Heaven. When such great lights have joined with you to give the little spark of your desire the power of God Himself, can you remain in darkness?

Seek for that door and find it. But before you try to open it, remind yourself no one can fail who seeks to reach the truth. And it is this request you make today.

Put out your hand, and see how easily the door swings open with your one intent to go beyond it. Angels light the way, so that all darkness vanishes, and you are standing in a light so bright and clear that you can understand all things you see. A tiny moment of surprise, perhaps, will make you pause before you realize the world you see before you in the light reflects the truth you knew, and did not quite forget in wandering away in dreams.

You cannot fail today. There walks with you the Spirit Heaven sent you, that you might approach this door some day, and through His aid slip effortlessly past it, to the light. Today that day has come. Today God keeps His ancient promise to His holy Son, as does His Son remember his to Him. This is a day of gladness, for we come to the appointed time and place where you will find the goal of all your searching here, and all the seeking of the world, which end together as you pass beyond the door.

Thank you for answering your call. The decisive imperative of your need to share your awakening from the *nothingness of this world* is much appreciated. I love you. -MT.

THE TWELVE STEPS

1. We admitted we were powerless over alcohol–that our lives had become unmanageable.

2. Came to believe that a Power greater than ourselves could restore us to sanity.

3. Made a decision to turn our will and our lives over to the care of God as we understood Him.

4. Made a searching and fearless moral inventory of ourselves.

5. Admitted to God, to ourselves, and to another human being the exact nature of our wrongs.

6. Were entirely ready to have God remove all these defects of character.

7. Humbly asked Him to remove our shortcomings.

8. Made a list of all persons we had harmed, and became willing to make amends to them all.

9. Made direct amends to such people wherever possible, except when to do so would injure them or others.

10. Continued to take personal inventory and when we were wrong promptly admitted it.

11. Sought through prayer and meditation to improve our conscious contact with God, as we understood Him, praying only for knowledge of His will for us and the power to carry that out.

12. Having had a spiritual awakening as the result of these Steps, we tried to carry this message to alcoholics, and to practice these principles in all our affairs.

A Personal
Awakening Experience

The only real, true method of teaching in the initial encounter, is the entire rejection of the conceptual association. Those of you who have been with me understand that fundamentally I have no interest in your erstwhile talents whatsoever. This is obviously Ramana Maharshi. My interest is only in you in the completion of your own process. That's just the way it is.

The necessity for that is very simply at the level of your heretofore consciousness association. You somewhere were in a presumption that there was value in the specific act of the creative purpose that you were using. It isn't that there was not value in it, but it would be almost impossible for you to express it in the fullness of your creative necessity without having it reflect to the gratification of your egotistical associations. I've never really tried to express that before, but I want you to see the evidence of it. Certainly if that energy procedure — let's use painting silk screen — certainly that well could end up in my association with you, at the minimum, cutting off your own ear. Are you familiar with that? Are you familiar with whopping off your own ear because you can't stand the limitation of your own creative mind? That was a physical happening of a very famous painter. The passion that I am offering you will be of such an intense nature that if I have directed you to a specific acknowledgment of your previous limitations, I would in effect be denying you the totality of your own mind. This is not open to discussion; this is a fact of the matter. This is what I do and what I am.

I have no real concern about what you bring me as to the nature of the manner in which you have become who you are in your relationship with me. It is not that it does not have value, but it only has value to the extent that you will admit that you are about to attempt to pursue a new course in which your own talents will be minimal, or progressively non-necessary for you. If you came to me, and I am speaking from my whole mind, and you said to me, "My name is so-and-so, I'm a doctor (or I'm a lawyer or I'm an Indian chief)." I am not concerned about it. My unconcern is what your salvation is. That's not true because I say it's true. It's true because I'm not concerned.

The truth of that matter is that I can't recognize human beings in their associations with themselves. I haven't been able to since my illumination. That is, I can operate on the premise that your name is so-and-so. I can be in the world and apparently participate with people with names, but I find no correspondence with them at all, and haven't since my illumination. It wouldn't mean anything to me. You could present me with any problem that you had, and while I would recognize it, I would not make an attempt to solve it within the association with you. That's just me.

How that came about is something because it came about. I'll use Wisconsin for a minute. I've never talked about this before. Obviously with what occurred to me, I had a full intention of being me, whatever I'm being right now. If I moved up, by some sort of miracle association, to a place in Wisconsin I call "God's Country Place," in no manner did I attempt to attract anyone. It didn't occur to me. I didn't know how to do it. If you would like an example of it, I have lived seven miles outside of a town called Reedsburg for ten years and I haven't spoken to anybody in ten years — it seems as though somewhere it never occurred to me — except to say hello. And this is a town that has seen little kids grow up and graduate, and I go in the same grocery store, and suddenly ten years has passed. And I'm not mayor of Reedsburg, which I would have been in about two years had I been my former self. So to me that seemed perfectly natural. It seems a little strange now because apparently I'm going to be able to say, "Hello." But in some manner I was accepted into the community. It isn't that people did not know that I lived out there, and I think the reason for it is that I didn't really pay any attention to them, so I was not a threat to them. There was no way that I became a threat, I simply lived there. That's the only way I can explain it. I drive a car that says, "Disabled Veteran." So they recognize me.

If you decide to go out and do this on your own, and you're going to cover your Christhood, you have to put up some sort of front association. This is just the way it will be. If I sent you on a mission here with a whole mind, I would expect you initially to garb yourself in a manner that would be acceptable initially in the attraction of the associations that were ready to hear you. That would be true whether you would be in Nazareth or wherever you would be.

The progression that has occurred in this has been expressed by an expanding willingness of the individual association who has been seeking the entirety of the solution to the problem. That's what I am offering. It would be very unlikely that, under any particular circumstance, this beautiful gentleman right here might care to listen to me tell him that there is no world, and that I am here to take him home with me, and that he is perfect as God created him. He wouldn't mind me telling him that I have a new way I would like to share my life with him. Or, I have a new way that I have discovered where you and I can go into business together. Or, I have a new church that I want to open up where we can attract attention. You would want to have me offer you a way in which you could continue to participate in your activities based on the direction that I would give you that would satisfy you in your own association with yourself. That's just the way it is. I don't do that. I don't know how to do it. My instructions to you are that this is not a real world, and you are going to get old and suffer pain and die unnecessarily. That's the fact of the matter. That's not open to a discussion as far as I'm concerned. Why would I open it to a discussion? I know the world isn't real. If you are happy to hear that, bless you. If you're not happy to hear that, bless you.

It could start out in a couple different ways. It could start out as a total rejection, in which case they won't hear me at all. I'm not threatening them with anything. The second thing will be, "How come this guy is so uncompromising?" You are accustomed in your own spiritual teaching to teach conceptually the possibility of some sort of illumination. The conceptual possibility of illumination is not what it is, and it is not what I teach. Your illumination, as far as I'm concerned, has nothing at all to do with your conceptual observation of it. If it did, you'd all be illuminate. You could be illuminate simply by judging yourself to be illuminate, which is the way most associations end up thinking they're illuminate.

The other factor involved in it is that it is impossible that I do not teach physical transformation because my transformation was physical. My transformation did not have to do with Christianity. It did not have to do with the doctrine of Zen. It did not have to do with the mystical horoscopes of the masters. My transformation was physical, because of the emergence in me of a solution that I found in a moment of revelation, that was explainable to me in my participation only under the new terms that I had found in that discovery. I really meant what I said, and I wish I could say it more simply than that.

You will have that initial experience, and this is called baptism, or the discovery of God, or an initial spiritual awakening. In my case, I was addicted to alcohol. I was addicted to everything. I was happily addicted to everything until I went into the hospital with cirrhosis of the liver. And I was still happily addicted to everything. So I couldn't solve the problem. I'm an example of a very successful problem-solver who isn't solving anything. That's the fact of the matter. I'm good at it. I was good at it since I was born. When that experience occurred with me, from then on all of my associations were based on a spiritual fact. Without explaining it to you, it was based on a spiritual fact that it happened to me and that it had entirely changed my life. I was relieved of an impossible association, one over which I had no control. (I'm talking about you, actually.) There was nothing I could do about it. Wherever I asked for help, or however that occurred, I'm not concerned about it. But from that moment on, I taught that there was a manner by which you could be relieved of any problem that you had simply by asking for help. How did I know that? I had had the experience.

I'll use the 12-Step Program for a minute, since I'm telling you how this worked for me. I discovered hundreds and thousands of other associations who had been in like conditions, who had undergone the same experience that I had. To me, that was astonishing! To me it was astonishing that I could go to a meeting. I'll use all of you guys: if all of us had come into this because we had overcome a single problem, we would immediately begin to share the overcoming of the problem rather than the problem itself. Have you got that? We would have in common — what? A spiritual experience that solved our problem. For those of you familiar with the 12-Step Program, this is exactly what the 12-Step Program is. Are you familiar with that? Who is familiar with Alcoholics Anonymous? Most of you have heard of the 12-Step Program. It is a spiritual program that says, "I am unmanageable. There is no way I can solve the problem. I'll make a decision to turn my will and my life over to God, and the problem will be solved."

But when I came together with associations, I discovered to my amazement that, to one degree or another if they were happy in their new discovery it had come about because of a spiritual awakening. Do you hear me? Is there a question on this? The reason that I teach spiritual awakening — and if this is too degrading for you I'm sorry — is because I was awakened spiritually from a condition that was no longer tolerable. That is really all I teach here today. There is no doctrine in that particularly, except the simple doctrine of forgiveness, very simply because the resentments of my association were what was causing my addiction — that is, my pain and inability to deal with the identities.

The twelfth step of the Program, which is *A Course In Miracles,* is: "Having had a spiritual awakening as a result of these steps, I practice these principles in my affairs and carry the message to other addicts." That's what I do. What began to occur with me in my necessity of service, I was taught not to judge the value of the service that I was giving, but only to give it. Who taught me that? I knew that if I began to take too much associate credit for what was happening to me, they would base their credit on me for their sobriety — which was not true since I knew that my sobriety (or my enlightenment) came from God, not myself. It isn't that I intentionally did the right thing; I did the right thing very simply because I knew that I was not responsible for my condition. Is that so, Program people? So when somebody said to me, "Boy, you're really good at this, how long have you been on the Program?" I said I came on this morning. Can you hear that? My response to that would be, I'm sober today, just like I'm telling you — today is the only day. I matured with teaching "one day at a time," which is what I still teach. What happened is that this began to fit more and more into a way of life for me.

The other thing that impressed me about it is that I was able to function at a very high level in the world, with an underlying acknowledgment of a problem that we had solved in mutuality in the world, without the necessity to acknowledge it to the world. I organized and had private Alcoholics Anonymous meetings where people would come who needed to maintain their anonymity. Can you hear this? This has changed. I'm going back quite a while — 25 years. If a man was desperate, and found a solution through the Program, and had to retain the anonymity — I could meet in an association with a judge or with a doctor or with a lawyer or with a clergyman or with anyone — we would meet and do this association with each other, and we could meet out in the world and acknowledge each other without the necessity to acknowledge it to the world. It is a lovely thing. They could trust me, or we could trust each other, to acknowledge our unmanageability and the solution through God and still operate in the world.

In that sense, your unmanageability can be unacknowledged. But somewhere you are going to have to acknowledge it to God and yourself and perhaps one other person. That's the fifth step of the Program. Somewhere you are going to have to tell somebody about all your problems. Maybe you're going to have to write them out. This is the Workbook of the *Course*. Do you understand? In the process, I could go out in the world; I was in the real estate business, and all that sort of thing; but we would meet and it was as though we had a secret association. You know why? We did! I would no more think of breaking the anonymity — it would be the last thing I would do. I wouldn't dream of doing that. If he wanted to go to an open meeting and stand up and give a talk, that was fine with me. But there was no way that I was going to disclose to the world that he had found peace and happiness through the grace of God. It is not that it did not change his life, and reflect in what he did in the world, but the world would not have recognized the totality of his unmanageability. Did you hear that? The world would not have recognized that the doctor botched an operation and killed a patient. Anybody could confess to me with the certainty that his confession had to do with the contrition of the realization of his recovery, not his determination to perform the fraudulent nature in which he is.

I was able to look at the fallacies of people and forgive them from the certainty that we're all fallible, and that the abominations that are going on in this world are incredible, and that no one really confesses to the other guy how much of that there is out there. This was the growth of my personal experience.

The only other element that's involved in it was my necessity to carry the message. Since I am a communicator, it's what I do. I'm a communicator. I'm a television star. I know how to do that. I grew up doing that. That's what I am. When I discovered *this*, I never lost my necessity to communicate it. I needed to carry the message. Obviously this is not different than carrying the message of anything. But for me, fortunately, it was carrying the message of — what? My spiritual awakening! So it turned into a necessity for me to serve. In other words, if somebody called on the telephone and somebody made a desperation call, the answering service would know particular people to call; I would get a call, and I would go out. So I went out in service and met all sorts of different people in all sorts of different circumstances. Everything from the worst dark alley you could ever find at 2 o'clock in the morning, to a big mansion up on the hill, with a guy who had given his wife a black eye — whatever it was. I would come up and walk in and sit with the solution if they were willing to accept it. So that's what I did. And I did it along with operating a business and all of that sort of thing.

Somewhere in that process I observed more and more people having an experience that I could see happening to them. There were occasions when I would get, say, the president of Sears, a real high executive who was totally unmanageable — dear ones, when I say totally unmanageable, I mean *totally* unmanageable — and no one knew it. If they knew it, they wouldn't even tell each other. Did you ever see a situation where the boss was so bad nobody even talks about it to themselves? It was like that. What a beautiful guy. And this is an example. I took him to Elgin. Elgin is our mental institution outside of Chicago. It's the worst place he could ever have been. And he came out of it the next morning, and he was sitting there in a chair with paper slippers and puke all over his bathrobe, and I'm sitting next to him there with my suit and tie, and he's just looking around. His situation... Folks, that's about as hopeless a situation as I have ever seen. He had gone from the mansion on the hill to suddenly sitting in this place with bars on the windows and blithering things around him, and here I am sitting next to him. And if you have ever shared a low point, those who have perhaps worked in this field and have had people experience low points, that point was about as low as anything that I have ever seen. That point was so low that it made the whole place low. It was just utter and total devastation, and I'm sitting right there with it. The difference was that I knew that in ten minutes I was going to get up and go out and get into my new Lincoln. I knew that I was out of it. So I was able to be in that situation — for all the reasons I can think of — including feeling the incredible compassion by my realization that I had been in the same boat that he was in. Do you hear me? What I'm really talking about is this: I had been in that boat, I had had that experience and I had had an experience that had overcome it.

I didn't counsel them. I never sympathized with people telling them they were drunk for all of the reasons. I never told them they were unmanageable because of their wife or their kids or their job. I told them they were unmanageable for one single reason, and that was ethyl alcohol. Just as I tell you you're unmanageable for one single reason: you are addicted to death — no other reason. You have one problem and I'm offering you one solution. I hadn't evolved that, but that's what it came to.

Then the miracle happened. Suddenly it began to turn. Those of you who have witnessed illuminations will recognize this. He suddenly began to raise his head and it was as though it had been dark and suddenly it began to get lighter. I don't mean that it got lighter with him. I mean it began to get lighter in the room. Can you hear me? Did you ever hear the story of Bill Wilson? Bill Wilson, the guy who founded Alcoholics Anonymous, was the worst that had ever been. And the description that the nurse gave at his recovery was that his whole bed was light. It was in 1933. It was witnessed! He was hospitalized for the 28th time, and they said suddenly when he had his experience there was a big light all around his bed. And of course that's what we teach. Anyway, it got brighter and brighter, and his head came up, like that, and it was just like that. The only thing he said was, "I don't have to do this anymore." What he actually said is, "I'm free." And he was. That was it. And in the decade that followed, he became one of the greatest teachers of the fundamental principles of the 12-Step Program without ever divulging that he had been there. He became very famous, calling on people of a particular nature who wanted to hear him.

What did he do the next day? He went to a beginners meeting. He began to make coffee, and he made the beginners meeting his home group. He never progressed past knowing that he had nothing to do with it. Good stuff. We have the kinds of associations that I see here, and I can see you, who know that you didn't have anything to do with this. Can you hear me? You knew that this revelation came for whatever reasons, not depending on you solving your problem, but on your inability to solve it. That's what happened to me.

The rest of my story: I began to have physical manifestations of awakening, as strange as that seems. I began to undergo genuine physical experiences that I had no way of defining, because I had had no experience with what a physical awakening was. Not only was my awakening physical, in one sense it wasn't particularly spiritual. You associate spirituality with Jesus appearing or with reading a scripture. That's really not what happened to me. What happened to me in the beginning was that I got a headache so bad I couldn't stand it. One of those! They took me in an ambulance to the hospital. I had a pressure in my head for no apparent reason, although somewhere I suspected that it might have to do with it, but I wasn't allowed to correlate it. They put me in Hinsdale Hospital. I was living in Naperville, 20 miles west of Chicago, a western suburb of Chicago. I had a couple of acres with horses out there. Boy, my headache got bad. A good friend of mine took one look at me and said, "You're going in the hospital." The pressure was building up, and they ran me through a CAT scan, and it appeared that I had some sort of tumor. Certainly I had pressure in my head, and my EEG was absolutely wild. It was off the scale. I was having seizures in the middle of my head. They sedated me and they said, "We're going to run some more tests on you tomorrow."

Here I am, under sedation, lying in this hospital in a private room, saying, "How the hell did I get here?" About 2 o'clock in the morning I was awakened by what appeared to be a passage of an energy association across the top of the room. I looked up at it, and it looked down at me and a voice in my mind said, "What's the matter with you?" And I said, "What do you mean what's the matter with me?" (This is in thought.) I said, "I've got this incredible pressure in my head." And he said, "Aw, don't worry about that, that's just a process." That's all he said. "Don't worry about that. That's normal. That's a process." Somebody had forgotten to tell me that. It was like my awakening (transformation) was accidental. And then it dawned on me. I said, "Oh, I'm in a process." And it was gone. All I had to do was make the admission that the occurrence was valid based on something that was happening to me. It began to connect spiritually, perhaps, but at that time it did not. The only problem I had was that I insisted on leaving

43

the hospital at 2 o'clock in the morning. It did not make the doctors and nurses too happy. "Where are you going?" "I'm leaving." "You can't leave here." I found my clothes. It was over and done. And, of course, I was fine.

And I began to have occurrences, and they were physical. My neck got burned, and my fingers all began to burn — all sorts of stuff, which was the sign of the awakening. And I was doing bizarre things because I was beginning to re-image in my mind. I had an image in my mind of a golden walking stick. For whatever reasons, I was shown a beautiful image of a golden walking stick. I didn't know what to do with it. So I decided to form the Peerless Walking Stick Company. The invention of my mind was that I would teach "spiritual walking." I don't know where this came from, but I would sell sticks, and we could communicate with each other by walking and talking, carrying a stick. I made the connection. I designed a beautiful brochure. And I wanted the heads to be beautiful. They were colored, and the 'finial'... I studied all about sticks. There's a great history of walking sticks. I decided I was going to import some special cane, *Ting Ling* cane it's called, which was the best cane you could get. But it came from Communist China. So I got on a plane and I went out to San Francisco. I was nuts. There's no question. For those of you who have had these experiences, it seems so reasonable at the time. And it was reasonable. So I contacted the agency out there for China, and I arranged to import cane. Actually, I did it. I imported it, and I sold a lot of sticks. So I had the Peerless Walking Stick Company.

So I was in downtown San Francisco for some reason or other, I must have been doing pretty well, and I was lying in bed. I had lived in San Francisco for ten years — in suburban San Francisco. I was at KGO in San Francisco in 1950 on television. Then I moved back to the Chicago area. So I'm up in the room, and I'm lying in bed, and all of a sudden I began to have genuine kundalini experiences. Starting at the bottom of my feet, voo-voo-voom, I *really* began to have them. And I knew nothing about it. Nothing. No one had ever told me that somehow there were chakras and about your spinal cord. It felt real good. It felt wonderful. I'm lying there, and it's kind of exciting. Some day I'll tell you about the passion I experienced there. I was not young then. I was a half a century then. You guys don't know how old I am. I'm older than you think. That's a long time ago. I'm talking about 17 or 18 years ago. During the awakening, I would have passionate experiences that were incredible, and they were based on absolutely nothing. You are accustomed to having some sort of passionate interlude that is justified by viewing a picture or seeing somebody. It wasn't true with me. I could be in the middle of a sales meeting and I had people working for me, and all of a sudden the energy would go voo-voo-voom!!

You could feel me — I'll tell you that. I learned very early to be very careful. I was taught to be careful because in the period I went through during my awakening, everybody would give me everything. And I didn't know why. But I could walk into the banker and he would try to loan me money. This is fun. I would sit down, smile, and say, "How are you doing?" and he would say, "How much do you want?" "I don't need any money." "Ah, come on." Something was going on.

And I would have passion. I would actually have total, full ejaculation passion. Oh, yes. They weren't pre-mature at all. In fact, they were very mature. That's kind of funny, isn't it? What am I doing here telling you this? I must be getting ready. My time is very short. Those of you who know me, I've never really told this.

I felt real good, and I was on Market Street in downtown San Francisco. I came out and walked down Powell or Mason. There was a little bookstore, one of the old kind in San Francisco, where there are all sorts of books. I always liked to go in them. They're kind of old-fashioned. And I walked in and

I was walking along, not looking for anything, and I glanced up just in time to have a book fall out and hit me on the head. That's a true happening. And I picked it up and it said, *The Kundalini Experience: Psychosis or Transcendence?* It was a book written by some doctor [Lee Sannella]. It actually fell out and hit me on the head. And I said, "Oh, that's what's happening to me! I'm in a kundalini experience. I better tell them it's not psychosis, that it's spiritual." It was probably more psychosis at the time. And that's a strange thing. When I say that happened, everybody goes, "Oh, no it didn't." But it did, although it seemed perfectly natural at the time. My certainty is that you are being guided in this. Like Jesus says, you may hear some very strange things, and you make some very strange requests, but it is impossible that you are not being guided, because you are under the same guide that guided me.

There is no explanation for my illumination, and as it continued, I was illuminate and my death process — what you call death, I don't use the term death — my devastation occurred on the 4th of July, 1979. Those kind of experiences are written about in books but they're not discussed. Obviously I was completely and totally devastated. Everything had been going so well. Everything was going just perfectly for me. I was happy with dogs and horses and my spiritual awakening, and I had begun to read books. I was in my bedroom, and all of a sudden it all caved in. That episode of fear could not be described. I didn't recognize it as death; it was preventing me from dying. There is no way that I could escape it. I tried to get underneath my wall-to-wall carpeting. I had wall-to-wall carpeting and I ripped up the side of the carpet and tried to hide underneath it. It was real interesting. The next morning I was entirely new. I was very certain, but I had no identification with my newness. I can remember about two days later (I was married at the time, and I had a child), we had company over to the house. We were entertaining, and I walked out into the living room (for some reason or another we were talking about the world) and said, "This world isn't real," and everybody turned and looked at me. I said, "Everybody knows this is not a real world." And they said, "What are you talking about?" I said, "The world isn't real. We're all here just doing what we do, and that's perfectly OK, but it's not real." And I began to have difficulties. Obviously.

From that time on, it's pretty intense. Your need to teach it will be pretty intense. So that's what I began to do. As far as the experiences themselves go, presume that they're going to be a part of your awakening. My instructions to you have always been, no matter what happens, no matter how bizarre, no matter how impossible, no matter how joyously happy, no matter how unpredictable they are, accept them as a part of the process, and you will be fine. If you read the preliminary statement in the Endeavor Academy *Out of Time* journal, it will say what I was taught about it. I was taught that it is an evolutionary process. These are direct teachings, and if you've read a lot of my old original writing (*Spiritual Teachers Notebook*), it will say this. The work I did in the first three or four years constitute very lucid descriptions of my mind that I was able to write, and took very much for granted. The idea that I could have done it a year before was absurd. Yet it seemed perfectly natural for me to do that, and I did.

The only explanation I ever got when they operated on my head... Suddenly my head was being operated on, and I could hear. Those of you who have ever had surgery and were conscious knew that the doctors were around you and you were lying in bed and they were operating on you. They were operating on me. Something was happening because I could feel it. And one of them said to the other one, "How's he going?" And the other guy said, "I don't think we can do it." And the other one said, "Why don't you try that?" And he said, "If you do that, he won't be able to see." And amazingly enough he said, "Well, go ahead, that's the best we're going to get." So that was performed on me. The reason I teach 'thought' is that I do not have visible light revelation. That is, I am not suddenly able to see light — or very rarely. If I share with some of my new associations, like you would be if you went to light suddenly, you might flash me some light. For me light is thought — dark light. There's really no difference in it, since light is thought anyway. I am able to think blue and give other people blue colors. But I don't see them myself. That, evidently, was the flaw that they said I would have in the procedure that I had. And that's the way it is with me.

But except for that, I learned it all by experience. We used the term "shakti" earlier. I didn't even know what that was. I didn't know that I had it. I didn't know why I went to Unity Church in Chicago. First I went to the Theosophical Society. I discovered Theosophy. The reason I did was that it is connected to Buddhism or kundalini rather than Christianity. My awakening wasn't connected to Christianity. It's kind of fascinating. I went downtown to the Unity Church, I walked in, and the minister said, "Why don't you give the service on Sunday." Those sorts of things have happened to me. In the middle of the service, the transcendental meditators who were sitting in the front row began to have very violent experiences in relationship with me. They began to fly. They had been to Fairfield (Iowa) where they were taught to fly with the Maharishi. They experienced my energy, and suddenly they began to hop way up. And it was a little embarrassing. They were sitting in the lotus position and all of a sudden they began to hop up into the air about 20 feet. And I said, "Oh, what's this? What's the matter with you?" And they were going, "Oh, Master!" They recognized me, even if I didn't.

The reason I couldn't be seduced was I knew damn well I didn't have anything to do with it. How would you seduce me? I got it through the grace of God and surrender and service. All I teach is serve. Give it away and serve. Holy mackerel! So that's what I do. That's pretty much my story. The voices directed me. My original nature was very protective; that is, I didn't even allow tape recorders in my talks. The early tapes that you hear of me were snuck in by a meditator underneath the chair. They're great talks. Some of them are as good as anything — in fact, they're probably better than I do today. For whatever reason, I protected that. For whatever reason, you are now interested in sitting and listening to me tell you this, which is a sign that there has been an integration of the so-called religious idea with the natural function of the emergence of you in a metamorphosis of your physical attainment. Yet it doesn't necessarily have to be connected to a doctrine, but it must be connected personally to a need or dedication to overcome a difficulty that is then overcome and maintained through service, forgiveness and love. That's what I do.

This association could perhaps respond to me in a moment for no reason whatsoever, simply because he would say, "That's what that is. That's the guy." Or they would hear about me and would say, "That's the guy. Where is he?" For no reason whatsoever — not because it had been prophesied. A lot of that happened. Some of you knew instantly that you were going to fulfill your function. It is very interesting that that did not necessarily have to be illuminating. Can you hear this? You could have a perceptual responsibility as a lawyer, or an accountant, or whatever you had to do; you would immediately come in and do that. Those of you who know how this grew will understand that. Some of you knew instantly you had to do that. And you did. And you are recognizable to me, generally by your determination.

What has occurred now for the first time began to happen at what we call time-sufficiency. In any particular association of space-time you reach sufficiency. That means that whatever the correlation of pain and death and chaos with our reality, there is a sufficient number that now justifies the exposure. I'll try that once more for you. My exposure is fundamentally very fearful. The *Course In Miracles* is the most fearful thing that could ever happen to you. It leads you directly into fear. The first chapter says it. That's why nobody does *A Course In Miracles*. The first chapter says this *Course* will lead you directly into fear. How could it not? It's the loss of your own identity. It's an experience of enlightenment. It's walking through the shadow of death. It's going into a Gethsemane. It's being crucified. It's being resurrected. It's all of those things.

Somewhere recently, there was a sufficiency of illumination that occurred in the ancillary association that has actually never occurred in the world before. Jesus teaches the idea of multiple saviorship, which is really what I'm expressing to you. That comes about simply because it is impossible to objectify me. I refuse your objectification of me. If I hadn't, I would now be the largest Christian denomination in the Universe. Had I set that up, if I had done that, we would have just been a gigantic establishment. But I didn't do that. I couldn't do that. I didn't want to do that. Why would I want you to do that? Instead I taught that you may do this through this process. And certainly that includes forgiveness and all the things that go with that. I never really taught forgiveness, I taught that this is going to happen to you. Give up and come to God.

Apparently, over a period of all these years, there is what we call a sub-culture listening to these tapes. They don't tell anybody. They just simply listen to them. What they don't really know is that it is accumulative. Each time anyone has an experience, and this includes the *Course In Miracles*, it affects everybody in that relationship. And those who weren't ready yesterday are ready today. I am able to do now, perhaps, with the formulation of the Healing Center, what I would not have done a year ago. To me the idea of healing didn't have a lot of meaning, because I could see everybody healed without all the nonsense of Christian healing. Not that I didn't love it and think it was good, but that was not what I did. I raised the dead. I was a teacher of teachers. I wanted you to come and do your own illumination. When that sufficiency occurred, we took it out into the world. This is directly from Jesus. If you take the *Course In Miracles* out into the world, take it out as healing because healing can be a physical demonstration of the spirituality without the necessity for the complete experience. Did you hear me? That does not mean you don't need the Academy or a place where you can come and complete your own process. But it does mean that you can offer to the world your healing grace through the energy of love that you have gained by your own transformation. That's what we do.

We have a Healing Center, and not very many people come to our Healing Center. But that's suddenly going to change because I'm healing. I am able to do it. So the contact that I make with you now is my allowance for you to accept me in partiality that I formerly never would have done. I'm just giving you the fact of the matter. Do you want to hear this? You can present me now with questions that before I would have said, "You're not listening to me at all, get out of here." That's why they say, "Don't go to him, he'll tell you that you're a dummy." Many of you, perhaps, are as dumb as you used to be, but perhaps not. That would be because of the sufficiency of the Light energy that has become a part of this. That occurs at what you call this level of association — coming from the medulla oblongata, and it actually occurs in the pineal gland. But instead of teaching simple reflection, I bring it from the pituitary, which actually includes the process from the gonads, directly to the pituitary. So my provision to you contains the Light and also the transformative possibility of your body. Did you hear that? I expressed that in the Eastern association. So when I offer you energy, you may suddenly experience more than you thought you would, simply because I'm an entire activator and am not limiting it to the upper few chakras. I don't know how to express that. That seems to be the case because you may very well begin to have very intense physical experiences.

More than that, this is a contagion of Light. You must understand that this is not all that big a place. There are only five billion of us. There's not that many of us. It's only a little place. When you begin to have the experience, everyone else begins to catch that Light in their association. It's a communicative ease. It can be communicated. In fact, it's easier to communicate than disease itself, because, when the resistance to it is relinquished, it is no longer necessary to set up other protective devices. The resistance of cause and effect is converted to the acceptance of it. In that sense, it's not remedial at all. It is the repair through the RNA to the DNA itself. There was no DNA here originally, it was RNA. The DNA is a formulation of the feminine association of potential. The message itself is carried by the DNA in the activation of the enzymes that transform your bodily associations contained within...oh, shut up! Who cares? But it *is* glandular. We keep getting calls: "Can I measure your melatonin?" So they've got melatonin and they are producing it artificially and they are using it as a sleep agent. Actually, it's a lot more than that. But since the body only accepts it as soothing, it will soothe. There's nothing wrong with it, but the activation could be very important to you in your own memory. That's all a part of the healing process.

Does that have to be explained to the people who come to be healed? No. But if I'm explaining it to you, it is probably an indication that you want to know about it. It is probably an indication that you are a teacher, or that you have a need to serve, or there is an element in you of service. I say "probably" because I have no way of determining it. Certainly, at this level of association, we need teachers. We need illuminate associations. But if they disappear from here, if they just leave, what good are they going to do us? Generally speaking, if you have an experience you will begin to carry that message or experience. The manner in which we intend to do this, as I told you earlier, is *A Course In Miracles.*

This is confidential. When I say I am communicating with Jesus, the mind of Jesus, directly, I mean it. I mean that the advice that you are getting is also of that. So let's stop kidding ourselves about the need to say who it is. I couldn't care less who it is. If it is an illuminate voice connected to what you have been looking at in the method of coming to know, which is the direct route — this route — that says, "Don't do anything. Come into this and it is available." Ramana Maharshi. The direct association of samadhi without any of the nonsense. At the very minimum with what you call Aurobindo — Integral Yoga, using your mind and letting yourself come to it. That's what I'm offering you.

Need you know this in order to be healed? No. That lovely mind back there is going to be healed regardless of anything he says. It is impossible that you can be around me and not be healed. But the joy that I'm beginning to experience in it is that there seems to be a very solid indication of a possibility that this association is about to be over. I'm going to say this to you in case you think that there is some way I can explain that. Let me try it this way: Over is over. I know that you think it ends in some big gigantic catastrophe. It doesn't. It simply doesn't end that way. Because of the nature of your spatial references, if there are too many of you, you will be viewed as an entire failure. Can you hear me? Outcomes are always predicted by what the associations want to see. I'll use the Healing Center. I invite everyone to a final association of the Healing Center and we all come and we say now the portal is going to open up and we're all going to ascend to Heaven at 12 o'clock tonight. Twelve o'clock comes and we ascend to Heaven and are gone. The next morning the people driving by in their cars say, "Oh, there they are, the whole thing failed." Can you hear me? It's the same as though I took twelve of you up to the top of the hill and say we're going to stay up here until God comes. The next day we come down from the hill all disheveled and it didn't work. That's nonsense. They left. You are the one that saw them come down. They're not here. They came down because they are phantom figures of failure in your mind.

It's the same people that saw Jesus crucified on the cross. He wasn't crucified. He's resurrected. Many of you didn't even want to accept Him when He came there and said, "I'm resurrected." Do you hear me? So your scenario is that of washing your hands. Your scenario is that of, "It didn't work." It would have to be, otherwise you wouldn't be here. Sorry about that. That sounds like a cop-out doesn't it? It is a cop-out. The one thing that you can't accept in the healing book, if you're really going to be a healer, is that your healing is perfect all the time. So this is a cop-out. You're going to use it perceptually to say, "Ha, ha, you failed." I didn't fail. When you read our *Miracle Healers Handbook* and it says, "Should Healing Be Repeated?," Jesus says, "What the hell are you talking about? It worked perfectly." It will then say, "Look at yourself." It will then say, "You don't seem to think that attempts to heal again are an attack on God." I don't want to get into it. That can't be understood by the world, and it does not have to be understood by the world. But it *does* have to be understood by you.

It needs to be understood by you because the conversion to phenomena will not solve the problem. It's not going to make any difference at all to the world — not really — if I go to Madison Square Garden and say, "At 12 noon today I am going to energize and disappear." I will do it. I will energize and I will disappear. And it will be good for a story for about three days. Am I right? "Man Disappears." Since it cannot be accepted into the entirety of the association, it becomes an anomaly. All of the definitions for how it occurred need not be true. There will then be people who say: "I saw him pulled out with strings." "It's not true." And all the other reasons why it's impossible that that occurred. If it is totally impossible, it won't be seen at all. Can you hear that? That's quite a step. If it is possible, but cannot be organized into the association, it will simply be rejected. It will not be considered part of the statistical possibility. Since I cannot die and I never get sick, I am not a part of the statistical possibility that organizes whether an 80-year-old man can get sick and die. I'm thrown out of the equation. You can't count me. I'll throw the experiment off. If I'm 460 years old, I don't count. Can you hear that? I can't be considered part of the association. Not that I am; actually I'm about 642 years old.

The persistence of the necessity of the conceptual mind not to acknowledge the miracle is amazing, because it must justify the association in the occupation of its own mind. A good friend of mine who is one of the best surgeons I ever knew, and he still is, and he is beginning to have experiences because I took care of a problem he had, confessed to me, that he was going to do a major stomach tumor (I mean major pancreas/stomach, no hope) surgery on a woman who had what the nurse describes as a spiritual experience the night before in the operating room. He didn't know about it, but they wheeled the woman into the room and the tumor wasn't there. It just wasn't there. Here are the possible reactions. First of all: "I've got the wrong patient." Next: "I've got the wrong X-rays. There must be a mistake in the X-rays." The pursuit of it finally becomes futile. And he looks at his watch, and says, "Well, take her away, I've got another one coming in." That's the way it works. That became an anomaly. Obviously, it was not acceptable within the association. I can share this with you. Of the many good doctor friends that I have, most of them know that their patients get better by miracles, not by how they treat them. I don't care whether you want to hear that or not — it's true. What they do is give them medication and pray. I'm talking about real general practitioners. I'm not talking about barbers. I'm not talking about surgeons. To me surgeons are barbers. Medicine is a craft and if a guy needed his leg cut off, he went to a barber because that's mechanical. You give them a remedy and you hope that suits them; and you hope that he recovers rather than killing him. Obviously, the remedy you give him is a poison directly connected to the healing — hopefully.

Actually, what happens is some doctors heal better than other doctors because they heal with their mind. GPs have a way — are there still any around? Are there General Practitioners? Some of them are quite good. We had a Dr. Layton who was so good all he had to do was show up. Not only was that true, but he knew it. He knew he had to show up, and he would pull up in his car, and get out with his bag and, "Oh, wow, you're finally here, doctor. I'm okay now." What was that? Service! It's nothing but service. It was a dedication. He wanted to make them well. He wished them well. He wanted to help them. His service was not based on monetary concern — at least not too much, not any more than necessary. So it wasn't a form of exchange, it was a form of giving or love. And that's the manner in which real healing occurs, isn't it? Your need to do that.

The intensity with which you are going to begin to express your love through giving is going to surprise you. That may become very passionate for you. This is Jesus. No one was more passionate or determined to teach revelation through the necessity to heal than that mind. So you will be an emulation of that mind. You will be a form of that mind, just as my mind is. I may sit here and begin to just talk to you about that because I want you to have that experience. There is some good pleasure going on concerning the breadth of the awakening that's occurring in this association. It's starting to show up on what we call the "Big Board."

I'm going to try a couple of things with you. This is not a real place. I know that you think somehow that you're spinning around. That's all well and good. But it's not really true. At any moment you may simply decide that the dream is over, and the dream is going to be over for you. I'm telling you that, as a fact of your own association. You should start to hear it. I know it is outrageous. I know it's impossible. I know it's mystical. I know all the reasons you can give me objectively for it. They have absolutely no meaning to me at all. I am speaking to you from a certainty that there is no such place as this. I almost immediately apologize for you being here, which is what I'm doing now. I'm sorry. I am sorry for this. I am talking directly to you.

I better tell you this: When I ask for an explanation of why I am able to do this without any apparent historic reference, I am told that I am a substitute. I am told that I am an insertion. I know this is true, if you would like to hear it. I am an insertion of a pattern of converting energy because your other savior didn't make it. I don't know how to explain this to you. But the assignment that was supposed to be performed failed. Krishnamurti appears to be who it was. At the time of the illumination of Krishnamurti, he was picked to be the connection between the East and the West, as I understand it. I'm just picking this up. He was spotted by Annie Besant. They saw him as a six-year-old and they saw his illuminate possibilities and he was taught to be the Christ. The problem that he had was that he was so fraudulently presented as the Christ. To be presented as the Christ when there is no verification for it in your own mind is not acceptable. And it just missed. Are you familiar with him? He's a beautiful, loving consciousness who, as I am doing now, would sit on the stage and say, "Look at it, look at it." But he could never offer his entirety. The rejection of that occurred at a carnival in 1936 when he got sick and tired of being presented as the Christ, particularly when he was being presented in a fraudulent manner, although that's the nature of it. I think that was Leadbeater and a couple of other guys. He absolutely rejected it. From that moment on he became a great spiritual teacher.

The energy of Krishnamurti probably would have lasted about 246 years because it was a step using physical transformation to include Christianity. To take the jump that you are taking with me to the actual physical resurrection of the body, and use the term "you must be born again" of 2000 years ago, is very difficult. But that's what I'm telling you. So the *Course In Miracles* is the outcome of that, and the *Course* said we're going to put this in now even though you're not ready for it. The *Course* actually says that. The situation is that you are missing a symbol that you can use to represent you, compared to Jesus, to model yourself off of. That's not there. So the *Course* was put in with the out-of-body experience of Jesus which is 2000 years old.

To try to make that connection is virtually impossible for you because you have no bridge for it. You couldn't use the connection of kundalini and awakening. That's what I am. I promise and guarantee you that although I'm using the faculties of a guy who was born and raised here, I am not from here. I am not from here. I can remember what this consciousness went through that justified or qualified me. And I can tell you stories about devastation — I was at the atomic bomb area after the bomb. I have all of that as part of my nature. But that's not the reason for my illumination. It is the reason why I was chosen to be illuminated. I was simply the most likely prospect. If you run everything through the computer (this is the way it works), you can turn up associations that for whatever reasons are justified in doing what they do. The stories that I have told you obviously qualify me. I saw my best friends killed. I killed other associations. I had battles, I had rage, I had passion, I was very young — on and on. And I'm old. I can remember these associations very well. That's why I have that.

So the memories that I present you with are human memories, but if you listen to me I positively am a ringer. The importance of that is this: Multiple saviorship will progress much more rapidly if you will accept a ringer, because there is no way that you can justify me in your historic reference. I'm not in it. So I can jump immediately to the necessity for your Christhood, which is exactly what I'm doing. I am not denying you the process by which I came to know it, but I am denying my

Christhood in relationship with the provincialism of what you are in becoming Christ. I look at you as provincial. I look at you as historic references of localities that are undergoing the experience. What are we going to have? Multiple saviors. That's at least 500 years off. And you are going to emerge very rapidly, that is, the idea in the *Course* where you would stand up and say, "I am the savior of the world," without using a model. You used me, but I didn't let you. You used me and all I expressed was my own certainty of your perfection. When I explained to you how I came about, I laid no claims to it being doctrinal at all because it wasn't. Isn't that amazing?

So in those first few years I went back and saw all of these things happen. What surprised me the most is nobody would accept what they were teaching. So I had to take what you had taught, and rejected and offer it to you anew simply because it was true. For me it is astonishing that you can now pick up the teachings of Jesus, which are so obvious if you would look at them, that everyone has denied for two thousand years, and now you can see it. The reason you can is that you are undergoing your own illumination.

I understand that you may well idolize me and that's perfectly OK. I'm going home anyway. You can now reject me and say, "Well, you didn't get it by any means; therefore I don't want anything to do with you, because I believe that it's necessary for me to have means to do it." If you ask me how to do it, I'll say things like serve, give everything away and let's get the hell out of here. This is Ramana Maharshi. I have absolutely no concern about the method that you come to do it. I will, if you will allow me to, provide you with all the necessary accoutrement of Light that will justify your leaving here with no necessity for any residual at all. You will not have to repeat it. Thank you!

Those of you who can hear this, here's what happens: Most of you are actually leaving and coming back. They don't know it; they may know it. When they come back they're just immediately in the association. I could leave here (and did just then), and come back any time I wanted, and it will be exactly the same time it was when I left. Can you hear that? It's like scribing the *Course*. When you turn it on, it's just going to keep right on saying what it's been saying for the last thousand years. It doesn't matter where it is; it will just pick up right at that moment.

If I pick up a lesson — these are the lessons of the Workbook — and I wanted to have a *Jesus Is Praying* book, this *Jesus Is Praying* book is invaluable. The *Miracle Healers Handbook* and all of them are wonderful things to have. I did the central thought for you. The central thoughts are: there is no world; there are no degrees of miracles; all power is given unto you; and the decision is yours. Isn't that fun? Here's Lesson 163: It says, "There is no death. The Son of God is free." Does that mean there is no death? It means there is no death and the Son of God is free!

Death is a thought that takes on many forms, often unrecognized. Is that so? Death takes on forms. *It may appear as sadness...* Is that death? *...fear, anxiety or doubt; as anger...* Is anger death? Yes! Any formulation of anything in your association is literally a denial of the perfection of your own mind, if you'd like to hear it. *...faithlessness and lack of trust; concern for bodies, envy...* Death is concern for bodies? He doesn't leave anything out in there. The only thing we want to impress on you with this is that you are dead. Every act that you perform, including what you think you love, is only love of death. Okay, we've got that. I'll finish it. *...and all forms in which the wish to be as you are not may come to tempt you. All such thoughts are but reflections of the worshipping of death as savior and as giver of release.*

There is almost no one in this room that somewhere along the line has not said, "I'll be glad when this is over. I've just had enough of this. I wish I was dead." So you go off somewhere and die a little bit and then come back and face the problem some more.

> *Embodiment of fear, the host of sin, god of the guilty and the lord of all illusions and deceptions, does the thought of death seem mighty.* Are you ready? Death is the lord of all illusions and deceptions.

Death is the devil of your mind. Death is what you bow down to and worship as a real, incredible power which can influence you. Do you see that? You are what? An advocate and an adherent of death. Obviously, death as God can have no power unless you empower it. Your advocacy of the devil, or death, is what death is. Death alone would be totally meaningless. Notice the difference between death and God. God is an eternal association Who is real despite your advocacy. I'm just telling you the fact of the matter. God is going to be God. He does not require a definition of Himself in correspondence. Death does. I'm giving you the fact of the matter. All you have to do at any moment in your mind is to say, "Death, I'm not going to pay any attention to you anymore." All of the forms that are apparently represented here are a part of the nature of death worship. We don't do human sacrifice much any more, do we? Do you still do human sacrifice? Sometimes you do. You don't eat each other any more, do you? You do sacrifice each other for love. At some high level, you sacrifice yourself to death, and "greater love hath no man than to die for his brother." And that's very valuable and it's very honorable because everything you do is honorable. But the fact of the matter is that it is to death. Finally, you're not going to do it any more. It doesn't make any sense.

The thought of death seems mighty. This is what got me into that little discussion with Gangaji. I really love her. I've got to clear that out for you. I don't want anyone to think I don't love Gangaji and Papaji. What I am teaching is obviously Ramana Maharshi. I do not want the advocacy — this would be true of Jesus Christ — of the association of any teacher of God to be reduced to a justification for death. Is that okay with you? I have to tell you this because I am told to do it. I don't know whether that bothers you or not. The same problem exists in Christianity. I don't want the Christian to tell me that somehow I have to die in order to find enlightenment; that somehow I have to model myself physically in a physical death association. Usually, where the problem will occur, and certainly it occurs with this association, is she will connect the need for ego death to the need for physical death. Obviously Ramana teaches, "I died." It had nothing to do with his body at all because from that moment on he said, "There is no world." If there is no world, the idea of body death is totally meaningless. This is *A Course In Miracles.* The idea that you would actually rot and get old and die is not contained anywhere in his teaching or in Jesus' teaching.

Here's what happened here. The association sees pain and death, which is the human condition. It also is teaching the teachings of Ramana, who says you must have a death experience, so she teaches that he had a death experience instead of a life experience. He may describe it as death, as Paul says, "I die daily." I die all the time. But that's not the expression of death; that's an expression of life. If it is an expression of death, it would indicate that death somehow has a power that can be asserted over you that is necessary for you to experience life — as though there is some sort of combat going on in you. It is not true!

What it results in is the necessity for you to accept in your mind that the loved ones that you are experiencing that are dying of cancer are necessary as a part of your own illumination. I can't accept it. That is not acceptable to me. It is just not fair. I understand that you're going to love them, but I cannot understand the necessity to get old and suffer and die in order that I may use it for the progress of my own awakening. The reason I had to do that is that I don't want anyone to be misled

— and certainly Papaji is not. Any problem these associations have will always be physical resurrection. And that doesn't concern me at all. This is a lovely little book. I had never seen it. She's beautiful. There's her picture, and she has a lot of lovely energy. But she says here, "I went to the funeral." She's talking about going to a funeral and having an experience of death. She says, "What you are speaking of now is sensing the power of death coming toward you." That is not acceptable to me. There is no way I'm going to empower death at all. "... the power of death coming toward you. Death is all around. Whenever there is birth there is death." I don't know what that means, but for me whenever there is birth there is eternal life. Sorry!

Here's the real problem: "A meeting with death is your opportunity." Her mother suffered a lot of pain and was dying. "This time with your mother can be a time of rejoicing." I couldn't. I can't. You can't sell me on that. I am allowed to have the pain that I'm feeling. I'm going to connect that pain to the reality of my transformation, but it's not going to justify it. "This time with your mother can be a time of rejoicing. Why else do you think death exists?" I don't know what that has to do with Ramana Maharshi. I'm going to tell you what it has to do with it: Nothing! "Why else do you think death exists?" So that we can witness it and justify the pain and the necessity to overcome it? I have no objection. There is no objection to teaching this. There is an objection coming from that entire cycle that says, "Don't teach that's what I say." Incidentally that came directly from Ramana who is my beautiful, dearly-beloved whole mind who teaches exactly what I'm teaching — and did, and does. "Why else do you think death exists? If there were no death, what a missed opportunity this would be to experience what does not die." I don't understand. "What is untouched by ill-health, birth, death, coming and going appearance. Death is a powerful utility for realization." Nonsense! Nonsense! Don't you believe that for one second. Don't you dare do that with me! Don't you dare justify death by telling me that somehow once you do that you're going to be able to experience. Don't you do it. Ramana says absolutely that death is impossible because this entire association is not what Life is at all. I was supposed to do that. That's the end of that. Bless her heart.

Question: You yourself said that your utter devastation got you to the point where you experienced the illumination.

That's what I am speaking of when I'm speaking of the death of the ego. But it has absolutely nothing to do with physical death. Her whole problem is that she has connected it with the physical death of the body. It is not connected to the body at all. It is the transformation of the body through the realization, not the death of the body. Is this what happened in Christianity? Sure. It's exactly the same thing that they're doing with Jesus in Christianity — which is fine. That objection came from a very high source. I'm not too familiar with those associations except as I meet the Eastern meditators' minds who are willing to look at me. Many of them are very joyous and they have lovely contacts of forgiveness and love. I would not want that to be the doctrine of their teaching, because it is not true. This is particularly important now, and then we'll end this. Don't empower death! If you let death have power over you, it will exercise it because you have given it the power to do so. Do you hear me? Death is an idea. You bet your boots it is. *Swear not to die, you holy son of God, you made* an agreement *that you can't keep.*

> *The frail, the helpless and the sick bow down before death's image, thinking it alone is real, inevitable, worthy of their trust. For it alone will surely come.*
>
> *Would you bow down to idols such as this? Here is the strength and might of God Himself perceived within an idol made of dust. Here is the opposite of God proclaimed as lord of all creation, stronger than God's Will for life, the endlessness of love and Heaven's perfect, changeless constancy. Here is the*

Will of Father and of Son defeated finally, and laid to rest beneath the headstone death has placed upon the body of the holy Son of God.

Unholy in defeat, he has become what death would have him be. His epitaph, which death itself has written, gives no name to him, for he has passed to dust. It says but this: 'Here lies a witness that God is dead.' "Because you are God's son dead.

If you are the perfect living Son of God; if you have allowed your brother to die, you are saying that God is dead. That is an amazing idea. *And this it writes again and still again, while all the while its worshippers agree, and kneeling down with foreheads to the ground, they whisper fearfully that it is so.* Yet the worshippers are never successful in dying. We can go to funerals. You and I can go and love each other and watch them lay our dear friend down in the grave. And we can say together what a wonderful association we had together. And that's all true. And now he is lost to us. And finally we are going to be lost in the same amnesia and death that's going to swallow us up. Dust to dust. Ashes to ashes. Till death do us part. Don't do that!

That doesn't mean that you don't go to the funeral. Go to the funeral and discover that he's standing right next to you. That's one of my great experiences. John O'Malley. How I loved him. He was a guy that didn't make it. He was an Irishman. He suffers from the Irish disease. No matter how many times he got it, he never got it. He just couldn't get it, and he finally just died of alcoholism. One of the sweetest, most wonderful blarney Irish guys — great joke teller. Of course all of the Program people went to his funeral. His mother was there. One of the alkies went up to her and said, "We're so sorry about John. Too bad he never got the Alcoholics Anonymous Program." And his mother said, "Oh, he wasn't that bad." Somehow he didn't really need the Program. And the guy was gone! It's typical of your defense against death.

So I'm standing there and all of a sudden he's standing right next to me. It was a real funny experience, because I must have called on that guy a million times. I bailed him out of jail. He had six kids. And he was a hard worker, but when he went, he would go entirely. Did you ever hear of being struck drunk? He could be entirely sober and everything was going along beautifully — the better it got, the more likely he was to have a slip — finally things would be going so good that he wouldn't turn into the bar, his truck would. He would swear to me that he went on by, but his truck turned in, and some other guy got out and went in and had a drink — but it wasn't him. In one particular sense, it wasn't him. Anyway, John was standing next to me, and he looked, and he said, "How do I look?" I said, "Just fine." What a lovely guy. He was never mean. When he was drunk he was the nicest guy you'd ever know. Wow! To be powerless and not be able to do anything about it is incredible. We've got you, guys, don't you worry.

It is impossible to worship death in any form, and still select a few you would not cherish and would yet avoid, while still believing in the rest. For death is total. Either all things die, or else they live and cannot die. No compromise is possible.

Life is eternal. What appears to be death is only a change to another form of life. Do you hear me? The change to another form of life that is occurring in you now is not death; it is Life. If it manifests itself as the destruction of the body within the form, be not concerned about that in your own relationship with yourself. It is indeed the resurrection. And that's the experience that you are having here with me now.

For here again we see an obvious position, which we must accept if we be sane; what contradicts one thought entirely can not be true, unless its opposite is proven false.

Once more, I don't want to make this hard for you since you are hearing me. There is an eternal loving Eternal Life. This is a place where there is pain and death. This is not real. That's why I want you to deny death. Why? It is not real. Any manifestation of space-time will be a form of a beginning and an end. Any manifestation. *In the beginning, God created Heaven and earth.* Is that so? When is it going to end? Never. Then why did it begin? I don't know. But anything that has a beginning will have an end. That's not what Life is, because Life is eternal. All of the other questions are valid: "How did I get here? Where am I going? What's going to happen?" I don't know. But if I can show you the simplicity of the eternity of Life compared to the split condition of your own mind, you can choose to be eternal, very simply because that's what you are. And that's the solution that I am offering you now in your own mind. Does it seem not to have any correspondence with time? It doesn't!

But what I'm curious about, if this is true, what possible connection would time have with eternity? Does eternity wait to be eternal until time decides it is? Jesus says that eternity is going on exactly the way it is when you made the sojourn into death. Nothing has changed at all. You came in, and you're going to leave, and you are going to be home. Won't that be nice?

> *Death's worshippers may be afraid. And yet, can thoughts like these be fearful? If they saw that it is only this which they believe, they would be instantly released. And you will show them this today.* And that's what I intend to show you. *There is no death, and we renounce it now in every form, for their salvation and our own as well. God made not death. Whatever form it takes must therefore be illusion. This the stand we take today. And it is given us to look past death, and see the life beyond.*

Is this what I said to read at all funerals? Yes! I got this to be read at funerals because it acknowledges eternal life at the grave site:

Our Father, bless our eyes today. We are Your messengers, and we would look upon the glorious reflection of Your Love which shines in everything. We live and move in You alone. We are not separate from Your eternal life. There is no death, for death is not Your Will. And we abide where You have placed us, in the life we share with You and with all living things, to be like You and part of You forever. We accept Your Thoughts as ours, and our will is one with Yours eternally. Amen.

Where did that come from? Do you know the guy that wrote that prayer? He's your best friend. He's standing right next to you now.

This story is about over. This is the story that will be told in space-time for the next thousand years. The story I told you today, I'm sure somebody is going to figure it out and tell the story. I don't care. They're going to discover this insertion, and they're going to discover the formulation of healing centers, and they're going to discover my lucid teaching of quantum in association with time, and all of the stuff that we have done together in our dedication to escape it, and it's going to become more and more commonplace in the nature of you coming from death to Life.

Sometimes at the end of these sojourns we experience a sort of nostalgia. It's like: Now that it's over, it was OK. All of the screw-ups and the stuff that we went through, forget it. All of the mis-adventures and all of the mis-communications. Jesus says in the *Course* that it's an incredible happening. It couldn't have happened, but it apparently did. I am happy to be able to report that the connection is intact. The reason that you can leave is because the function of the completion of the association of resurrection, or a path from time to eternity, is becoming available.

First of all, what we did was establish a fast lane because of the clog — the slowness of the super-highway, what you call the "King's Highway." It just clogged up because no one was entirely sure that they wanted to go to it. If you don't have clear vision up ahead, you have a tendency to take one step up and two steps back. So the highway has been clogged up. Generally speaking, the first thing we did was give you a fast lane where you could drive along the outside of it. That did not complete the process, but it enabled you to go up the side, at least get ahead of 500 years, get out and begin to direct traffic to get out of the way for those who were being clogged up by the associations that didn't want to hear this. Or, perhaps, to invite some fellow travelers, who wondered what the hell was going on, to ride up with you and come out and take a look at the result, because they could see immediately that getting in that mess wasn't what they wanted to do. That's a fact. I don't know how else to explain this. I'm just talking energy here.

The other answer was to evolve, as some of us have, simply another way out. You may believe that the only way out of this is the King's Highway. That is not true. There has always been available in space-time continuum what we call worm holes, or methods by which you can move directly through time to another association. We used to think of them as back doors that we would climb, or places behind other associations that we could go to. So some of you have learned methods of literally disappearing from the earth for as long a period as you want to, and then returning to fulfill a particular function. This is going to happen more and more in this world as more and more of you become necessary in specific reassociations for specific jobs. You may call them angels if you wish. They are a step above an angel because they are fully facilitated to perform any act necessary, where an angel is a thought of a particular necessity that is expressed by your desire in limitation. What it says is this: If you are at any moment ready to meet the Christ, He can appear for you around the corner as a peanut vendor, and rather than having to offer you a bag of peanuts on the house and communicate with you something that you are ready to hear, which is what an angel would do... If you came around the corner and needed to know something, somebody might suddenly hand you a slip of paper. Obviously it would be an angel that's offering you a solution. It's very possible for you to meet your own association that's telling you directly that it is time for you to do this. It is time for you to take your place as the savior.

Obviously what I'm trying to do is express what is not expressible. But it is 'experienceable,' and certainly any story that you want to tell about it is fine with me. It will be a drama of you coming here, being here and coming home. And it will include the method by which you came home, even though the method is not real and requires a recognition of you individually. How else would it be if God is in everything you do and always present? You must be shown that in a method that is acceptable to you. And that's what we are doing now.

At The
Miracles Reunion:
A "Closed" Meeting

[Chuck A.:] I'm going to read *How It Works*. Hi. Hello. My name is Chuck Anderson. I'm an alcoholic. [Hi, Chuck] I've asked permission for the camera to be present in this closed meeting. The first thing I'll say is I will, of course, respect your anonymity.

The feeling of a closed meeting of Alcoholics Anonymous is present in this place, and I can feel it. If you'll tolerate me for just a few moments, I've been around since early this morning, and I've put together a considerable number of 24 hours, whatever in the hell that means. I know it means this, I know it means that the feeling that I am having right now is *exactly* the same feeling [I had] the first time that I walked into a meeting. I mean, not necessarily the first couple of times -- I was too drunk to have a feeling!

In those days you used to be able to go to meetings when you were drunk. I've been around -- I don't know -- a long time. Anyway, there weren't a lot of rehab centers. They were just starting. And, you know, if you didn't go to a meeting drunk, when were you going to go to one? You were always drunk, anyway. You had to learn to shut up and not be obtrusive in the meeting. But certainly, if I went and called on a guy, or they called on me, I was drunk. I called the answering service, and they came out as a group to see me, and I was drunk. But I wouldn't have called the answering service unless I were sober or had such a terrible hangover or just got out of jail or something. There would be some reason.

So the first couple times I went to a meeting, I was drunk. But the first time that I suddenly realized that it might be possible for me to actually not indulge in altering my consciousness, that is, not in my continuing long-term dependence on "Mr. Feelgood" or on a way that I could relieve how I felt, was in the presence of those who shared with me that experience. Somewhere I was able to say at that first meeting, "I'm where I belong."

And for those of you who have had, and share with me the experiences that I would admit that I needed Alcoholics Anonymous, and if there was one thing I knew that I was going to be able to deal with, it was my addiction. The idea that through the admission of my total inability to deal with my problem was the solution, is how I found this program.

One of the reasons that I wanted to talk to you as beginners is first of all, I feel myself as a beginner. There is no manner where, when I just felt the relief that I felt of being able to share with you a common problem in which we found a common solution, I was not happy about it. But I've been looking a little bit, and I don't want to digress from our necessity to look at each other in our association, but in the time that I have spent in the program, the fellowship of Alcoholics Anonymous, I observed over a period of these many years continuing deterioration in the manner and method by which our sobriety has been achieved. And I intend to talk about it.

And I may end up, with your permission, talking just a little bit about some of you there — I'm talking to you now —

who find yourself incarcerated in a penal institution, where there are indications statistically that in this country 80% of all the young men and women serving less than ten years in institutions are there because of drug-related problems. Is that true?

Even higher than that? 102%, But I want to talk to the guys for a minute about it. And the reason maybe they'll let me talk to them is because — which is true of you guys — you can't con an alkie. A guy who has been successful in overcoming the incredible need to alter his consciousness because he can't stand himself can understand perfectly well the dilemma being faced by young addicts who began at early ages to sedate themselves and have never actually faced the problem that everyone in this room finally addressed. And *that* was that their problem *was* the booze.

All right, I'm going to say this to you, and the counselor next to you is going to say, "Yes, I know but…." You listen to me, you guys. You have one problem. And this is how I got this program. I could give you every excuse under the sun for why I had to hit a cop and get locked up in jail. The fact of the matter was, I was drunk. Or I can give you every excuse for why I couldn't remember what I had done when I woke up and my car was parked in the garage. I had hung up my suit and went to sleep and woke up and I had absolutely no recollection of it.

So I struggled for a long time with what anyone in their right senses would have recognized immediately as unmanageability. Do you hear what I'm saying, alkies? I know you share this. How do you measure unmanageability if you continue to function? How do you measure unmanageability out there in the street when your entire society is depending on the drug to justify the association, yet they're not in jail and you are?

Now, you'll use all…. I'm talking to you there. You're going to use all the excuses that you are offered by the court for the crime that you committed for which you should be punished.

And they will include your personal encounters with your family, with your friends, being deprived, being in poor associations, having needs for other things you couldn't find, being part of a lost generation.

You listen to me, you guys in jail. That's nonsense. You are there because you're an addict. You are there because you are powerless over the drug you have been using. No other reason.

I don't want to listen to this con job about "If that hadn't happened, I wouldn't be there." That's not how I got this. I didn't quit drinking because I got cirrhosis of the liver. I quit drinking because I couldn't manage my own life. Cirrhosis didn't stop me from drinking. I drank with cirrhosis.

Did you ever hear of Adabrin? Not Adabrin but Anabuse? [Yes] Did you ever try it? Did you? If you take Anabuse, you can't drink. So what's your solution? Don't take it. If you try to drink with Anabuse, I've got news for you.

I'm digressing a little bit. But you guys, you listen to me. Everyone in this room knows that the fundamental teachings of the spiritual program of Alcoholics Anonymous says you have one problem. What is it, Michael? [Booze] What's the solution? [Don't drink] Don't drink.

Now, to a guy who was like I was, who literally lived to drink and subsequently drank to live, or the guy that has no knowledge of what the world is like and is doing five years for drug abuse, he cannot not believe that his unmanageability can be attributed to the fact that he got caught and arrested and put in jail. Perhaps that is the case. But that is not the solution that I am offering him, and I am speaking from the experience of an addict. And you listen to me.

Addicts? You're different. Half the guys in your gang are never going to go to jail because they do anything. Many of the associations who for a period of many years I drank successfully with are still drinking successfully. I couldn't. That's how I got this. Say, "Of course." [Of course]

Now, obviously, this is what this says. This says that "Half measures are going to avail us nothing, and we must admit that we are powerless over the drug," and this goes back to a lot of letters we are getting from those who are incarcerated. You're in jail. And what brought it to my attention was a news program a couple of days ago from a warden who would not approve a program of recovery in the jail. And the reason he would not approve it was very interesting. He said, "They're incarcerated. They can't drink, anyway. Why do they need the program?"

Shame on you, Warden. Oh, yeah, that's very common. "As long as they're going to be in for five years, why give them a program?" What that is is a misrepresentation of exactly what the program of Alcoholics Anonymous is. The program of Alcoholics Anonymous is to teach you a new way of thinking, you that are in the prison, to show you that there is a solution to the necessity for you to shoot up or consume drugs that has nothing at all to do with the actions that are out there but your certainty that you don't want to do it anymore, and that through a spiritual determination, through the steps of this program, there is a solution, as unacceptable as the language may be to you.

As your sponsor, I offer you this: my certainty that if you're incarcerated and you think you might be an addict, you are. Just as when anyone in the world questioned me about whether they were alcoholic, I was virtually certain that they were. There are very few people that really address the idea that they are alcoholic without hiding their need for a couple of doubles in the morning.

So the solution that I have offered and been successful with is, very simply, my determination that I couldn't solve the problem. And I couldn't solve it because I'm an addict. And under all circumstances, given the opportunity, I would consume alcohol. The idea that I could live my life — I'm talking to you in jail — for many of you who have really

75

looked at it with me, the idea that I could live my life without the sedating effects of alcohol was impossible for me. Those of you who are in the jail, the idea that you would be able to go out and face the world without consuming or without redefining your problem through the use of drugs is very difficult for you.

What I'd like to see happen, and with the help of the guys that are in this room, we intend to inaugurate programs where we can bring back the fundamental idea that the solution to your problem lies in turning your will and your life over to the care of God. That in no way implies that you have to have some sort of "title" for how that's going to turn out.

I've seen many a guy — I'm talking to you in jail — who declared Jesus Christ to be their personal savior and got thrown in jail two days later for being drunk. If that offends you, Christians, I'm sorry. I'm not dealing with the doctrine of Christianity through Jesus Christ. I'm dealing with your inability to manage your own situation, with my certainty that if you don't drug, you can overcome it through a means that we can offer them; that the solution will not only change your life, it will make you happy in the change, because you'll realize that the endless cycle that you were in required that you drug in order to solve the problem that was caused by drugging, and it's an endless chain. Is that true?

I don't know if I'm making any sense to you. I'd like to sponsor you. And write us with the names of everyone in this room that would like to take on the idea of offering you a continuing solution while you're there so that you'll begin to apply the hope and faith that we discovered in a solution that was available to us.

I don't know how much sense that made, but I can assure you of this: I've walked in your shoes. You guys that are locked up? I've been locked up. You guys that are told you're insane? I was told I was insane. Is this true, Morgan? [Yes] There's not anything that could occur in society that all of us in this room had not found the solution through the Alcoholics Anonymous program.

So when the counselor begins to tell you about all the other problems you have besides the booze, the drug, you say, "I don't believe that. I believe that if I don't drug myself, I'm told by successful programmers who have overcome this disease to a faith and a dependency on a Higher Power that if I don't drug, all of my problems will not be solved but they will be solvable. If I drug, I'm never going to be able to solve them, because they'll be retained by my inability to deal with them because I drug, yet I need the drug in order to deal with them." Is that true?

It's a vicious cycle, and my escape from it, or the discovery that coming into this room, you would be willing to share with me your story of unmanageability where we could correspond with each other the manner in which we found the solution, which is how it works through this program....

Rarely have we seen a person fail who has thoroughly followed our path. Those who do not succeed are unable to give themselves entirely to the program. Perhaps they are constitutionally incapable of being honest. You listen to me, guys. There are a lot of counselors in there who are going to tell you you're never going to make it. Don't you believe them. They depend on you requiring sedation in order to counsel you.

And that's enough of that. Hopefully, I've got you to see that you have one problem and one solution. It makes it so simple. My sponsor said to me, and I was giving him all the reasons.... I've got more reasons why I had to drink than.... It's cunning and baffling.

And the other thing I had to learn that you taught me is that any measures that I employed except the uncompromising determination not to, would not succeed. Half measures availed me nothing. I could cut down. I could say, "No, I'm not going to." I could employ all of the techniques that work for everybody else. What I'm telling you — and what we discovered in this room — is it wouldn't work for us. At that point we looked for others and found them — and this is the founding of Alcoholics Anonymous, of those who shared our problem, and had found the solution in the manner in which we found it.

What does it have to do with counseling? Nothing. The discovery that there is a Power greater than myself that would restore me to sanity was an amazing discovery. I can remember waking up.... You share this with me in jail. Tomorrow morning, when you wake up, understand that you have plans for a future that will be different than what put you into the institution. Then gather with those who want to share your plans of overcoming the problem through a new way of thinking, an ability that you can evolve to find a solution.

It will give you more than the ability not to consume; it will give you a self-confidence through your capacity to overcome it that you heretofore had not experienced. Is that all right? [Yes] That's what you read today in the Twenty-Four Hour Book. All power comes from God, and the admission that you can't solve the problem is the admission that He will solve it if you let Him.

Now, I don't know how the offering for tonight and this talk is different than any AA meeting, except it seems that the last one that I observed in attendance, they were all losers. This program says, "I have recovered and am sharing my recovery." It doesn't say, "We came together to share our unsolvable problem." There's nothing in Alcoholics Anonymous when I attended that didn't say, "If you follow our instructions, you will recover." One day at a time. If you'll get up in the morning and say, "Today I'm not going to drink. My problem is booze. I'm going to read my Twenty-Four Hour Book. I'm going to share the solution with a couple of phone calls during the day to reinforce, should I be tempted."

And I found that it worked. And I'd been around for a long time, working it a day at a time, because those of you who are incarcerated and certainly those in this room have discovered that working your program or your life intentions a day at a time has made you basically happy, and carrying the grievance of your old intentions that necessitated your sedation no longer tempts you, because when you get up in the morning, you're starting anew. That's the basis of this teaching. Yes or no?

All I'm telling you and reinforcing with you, you there in jail or you in jail in your law office or you, doctor, in jail behind your little shoot-ups you're doing, don't kid me. You maintain that you are not unmanageable, where in your heart you know you are. And you're going to spend twenty years proving that you're not, because you feel the stigma of the admission of your inability to deal with the problem. Yet nothing will give you more joy if you'll come and share with us your inability to deal with it, because we can show you that through our inability, through our surrender, through our recognition that there was no alternative, we found the solution.

We don't say, "Amen," at Alcoholics' meetings.

Yes! I live with the solution. And if you're in jail, you can begin to live. I don't care whether it's Jesus Christ. What it is is a Power that is utilizable to me that will relieve me of the necessity to consume alcohol or to drink.

And you guys that are jail, I know that the drug has a different effect on you (particularly if you become more unmanageable) than it has on the people in the gang with you. All the more reason why you must admit that you can't deal with it. That has nothing to do with how happy it made you. It has nothing to do with the relief it gave you. I'm aware of that. As a matter of fact, it gave you more relief than it does the other guy, because you *needed* more relief. Okay?

I want you to see that that admission, that you can't get along without the drug, will help you and that we will help you in the certainty that there's a Power greater than you that will restore you to sanity, and that the help of your determination, when you are released, to go out into the world with that security and seek out others, whether in penitentiaries or attending programs daily or weekly, with the certainty that they have found the solution, will make you indescribably happy.

It's like a new lease on life. It's like a discovery that you never thought you could experience. It's like a realization that "I know I can't do what I'm doing, yet I can't stop. I'm desperate. What am I going to do?" This is your solution. Stop comparing yourself with the world. Compare yourself with us. We understand your problem. I understand your problem. Do you think that everybody in this room doesn't know, when they needed a fix, they needed one? Do you think that we don't know that the counselor or the judge or whoever else is going to say, "What's the matter with you, young man? Why is it that you need this?"? You need it because you're an addict. You're different than whatever you think "normal" is. In our minds there's no such thing as "normal."

We are very certain that there is a Power in this universe that will help us if we ask, and that the problems that we have been unable to deal with that have caused us to seek solutions in drugs can be well-addressed and overcome by not using the drug. And if that's difficult for you to understand, keep going through the cycle, because everyone in this room knows that through this program they have found the solution.

What does it require? An uncompromising admission that your life was not manageable. An uncompromising admission that "Something is fundamentally wrong with me," that "I can't solve this problem." It's a coming — with our assistance — to believe that a Power greater than ourselves will restore us to sanity, where, before we commit the willful act of violence in order to obtain the drug, or under the influence of the drug, we will say, "Wait a minute. I am aware of the consequences that will occur" — not because of the act but (in the vast majority of cases) because of the connection with the drug. All right?

Made a decision.... Make a decision to turn your will and your life over to the care of this Power, as you understand it, a decision to say, "I can't deal with this," an *act* of surrender, so that when somebody says to you, "Why don't you buck up?".... No one in an AA meeting, in a genuine 12-Step meeting will say to you, "What's the matter with you? Why don't you buck up and deal with it?" They will be of a fashion where we share together our unmanageability.

The joy that I felt when I came into this room was the sharing of a bonding, the sharing of a common solution, that those of you who are in the penitentiary, when you come out and go back into your daily lives, if you're accorded the faith in this program, you'll suddenly discover others who have had the same experience. And we want to activate a spiritual program called *A Course in Miracles*. It's not called *A Course in Miracles*. It's called the Alcoholics Anonymous program.

For those of you who don't know where we're speaking, we're at a Miracles Healing Center, where, beginning with turning our will over to God on a continuing basis, offering our service to you as I continue to do and we all do, I find, as we have found on the program, that in order to keep the solution that we discovered, we have to give it away. That's called the Twelfth Step in this program, for those of you who are not familiar with the program. So the Twelfth Step is saying, "We must carry this message in order to enhance our ability to see that we have found the solution through this program."

Now, the beginning of *How It Works* (and this is all past tense) will include passages like *With all the earnestness at our command, we beg of you to be fearless and thorough from the very start.* Half measures availed us nothing. One shot, one booze, will make us powerless again.

Once you get the hang of this, you'll discover that it gets easier and easier, because the alternative to not drugging will open doors to you that were previously not available. Young guys? Those of you who have never really had a life without the sedation, if you are incarcerated now, find a counselor or we'll come down there. You call us. There's a jail now in California that we're liable to send some guys in. We want to sit down and talk to you, dudes.

You think that somehow you're going to go out and face the same problem. We want to show you that if you find the solution here, for all the reasons that you've been in here, you'll not repeat them when you go out into the world. Why? You'll have found a solution. Is it a spiritual solution? Yes. Were you powerless over the drug? Yes. Did you find the solution through turning your will and your life over to God? So that's how it works. And *rarely have we seen a person fail who follows our path. Half measures availed us nothing.*

Where you're standing right now, if you want to share this with me — and I'm your sponsor — is at the turning point. You ask for *His* care, this Power, with complete abandon and you'll have the solution, simply because the problem will be solved. And that's a miraculous discovery. And it's a discovery that I made. And it's a discovery that I have been persistent in over a considerable number of 24 hours of sharing with you. And I'm sharing it with everybody in this room right now.

With the maturity of my program in the discovery of the Power, new doors were immediately opened to me, because, first of all, I didn't constantly need to sedate myself in order to justify myself. Those of you who drank successfully, as I did for many years, were always told, "He's going to be all right" or "He can deal with it" or "Your problem is not really heroin. Your problem is get some counseling for your old man beating you." Don't you believe that. Don't you believe that. Your problem is the drug.

I remember my sponsor saying to me, "Don't be ridiculous! You know perfectly well that when you take a shot, you feel a hell of a lot better than you did before. And the idea that you didn't is just crazy. Of course you felt better."

"Well, then just have a couple. You'll be all right. No, just get a little fix."

We all laugh together because we're addicts. And you, out there, you're in jail. Obviously, there may be twenty guys in your gang that do it once in a while that are holding jobs and are very successful. That's not you. And the admission that's not you and that there is a group that understands your problem is going to make you very happy, I think. I hope so.

I don't know whether the age difference and the counseling that you received about the nonsense of various solutions.... But if I can show you that everybody in *this* room is certain that their new-found freedom is based on this program, they won't be offering you a variety of capacities for you to deal with your alcoholism.

I don't need to be told there's other methods where you can stay sober. I'm not interested in that. The manner that I'm offering you I know works. And it may also be the manner that's the most difficult for you because there's no compromise in it. *Half measures availed us nothing. We stood at the turning point. We asked for His care and protection with complete abandon. Here are the steps that we took* — past tense — that offered us the solution.

So we're gathered here at this Miracles Healing Center because we're miracles. And we're sharing with you, there, wherever you are, our certainty that this program works. What did we do? We admitted we were powerless, we believed that there was an alternative and we made a decision to turn our will and our life over to the care of God.

And now, suddenly, there you are. You're in the institution, and you've decided you're not going to do it anymore. Do you have time to take an inventory of all the things that have caused you to drink? You have plenty of time to do that. Your emphasis doesn't have to be on your inventory. It's perfectly proper for you to review the things that you have done and let them be based on what you really were searching for. And then this program will have a great deal of value to you.

We made a fearless moral inventory of ourselves and *We admitted to God, to ourselves, and to another human being the exact nature of our* difficulty. [This is] the idea that you could actually share with another human being and our Creator and yourself the fundamental problem you have in dealing with what the world has told you that you are and that you have accepted, necessitating your need to drug as justification for what the world told you that you are. And the world is wrong.

Young guys in there? The world is wrong about the situation that you find yourself in. The power of decision is in you. Initially it's the confrontation with your inability to deal with the drug, very simply because your problem is the drug. That's what we share in this room, no matter what happened to us. Half of us have been in jail. Half of us have lost our families. Many of us have gone through experiences that very much associate with yours.

Our solution came from admitting we had one problem. Did it solve everything? No, but it opened a door for us to examine what our problems were, with a capacity to look directly at them and see that the world couldn't set terms for our solution if the confidence we have gained through this program could be enhanced and brought more to our attention.

You guys out there? Don't underestimate the power of your new-found capacity not to drug. There isn't anybody in this room... And I'm not concerned about what the world tells you. The world's going to say, "Oh, that's easy to do." It's *not* easy to do. And we can share with you the problem that you had in solving this problem. And that's why we have a program called Alcoholics Anonymous. Okay?

So we're going to share our experience and our faith and hope with you. And wherever you are, watching or listening to this video…. And we're directing it particularly to institutions. Obviously, anyone who is powerless over booze and hasn't admitted it has imprisoned himself in a hopeless situation that he does not admit to the world. And there's a lot of you that I'm looking at right now that intend to spend another ten years dealing with a problem that you really can't solve. And it's going to constantly reduce your capacity to really address the true nature of what you can do. And that's too bad, because you are handicapped by your need to sedate yourself.

Judge? Doctor? Lawyer? You can't fool us. We're a fellowship that gets together and admits in this inventory of what we did and the guilt that we feel. But we understand that through our new-found capacity, through our surrender to a Power greater than ourselves, we have found the solution.

These are the steps of the Alcoholics Anonymous program, and all of you, virtually all of you out there, are familiar with them. But I doubt very much if anyone has really told you that this works. All around you are evidences of the failure that it will. You listen to me. It works. It will work. And it's the only thing that will work for you. This program is the only thing that's going to work for you. Is that true for us in this room? [Yes] Is that too uncompromising for some of you?

Those of you who…. I don't know how long you've been around. "Well, there's probably another way that I could have found it." That's pure bullshit. The way you found it is this. You found it through a Power greater than yourself, not through your decision-making capacity. That's nonsense. Those of us who have tested our decision-making capacity over a period of many years are very certain that's not how we got this program. That's not how we obtained this happy sobriety. Did I do them all?

…admitted to God, to ourselves, and to another human being the nature of our wrongs; were entirely ready to

have God remove all these defects of character; humbly asked Him to remove our shortcomings. We made a list of people that we had harmed. As long as you're doing penance, you can call them up and say that you're not going to do it anymore, and don't be afraid to talk about the program. Tell them that you discovered a new way to live that you intend to employ when you get out of the hoosegow. Do you still call it the "hoosegow"? The "klink," or whatever you call it.

The other thing you'll discover is that if you look around, you'll meet associations in the penitentiary that actually share your problem. They're going to express it in a lot of different ways, but the fact is, there's something about the nature of you that makes you unable to deal with the world on the terms that the world requires that you deal with it.

And the doors that will be opened to you when you leave the institution based on this program will be so amazing that you won't believe it. I'll tell you one reason: We'll find you a job. If you work this program — and we can tell — and you come out of the place that you're in, we'll find you a job. And we'll say, "This guy did this in there. He's determined to change his life." Many of us found jobs that way. You know that, and I know that. What could be more down and out than somebody that's where you are, or is somewhere where we were, whether acknowledged to the world or not?

Is it a second chance? You bet. Will it change your mind about yourself? You bet. It's a surprising thing, and the happiness that I want to share with you is my certainty that the feeling of despondency you have right there, now, is exactly what all of us felt, whether we were in jail or not. We were in a jail that we could not escape from and we could not share with the world, just as you are. *Bars do not a prison make.* What's the next line? [*Nor iron bars a cage*] Nor what? [*Iron bars a cage*] Or *iron bars a cage.* Thank you, John. Oh! There's John back there. He's an alkie. One of my old boozing buddies.

You'll discover in the admission of your unmanageability.... And I suggest this to you: Do it with anonymity. That means in confidence with each other. That way, you can talk about anything, and we have a responsibility not to disclose it to the world, because we're sharing the solution, not the problem. That doesn't mean you don't tell us about the problem. We know you have problems.

I don't know how much value this will be to you. I know this: These guys gave me a chance, and without this meeting there was no chance for me. Am I all right with that? [Yes] Without what occurred to me, sitting with you, I was hopeless. That's what this says. It requires the experience, and it requires your determination to work it. And it's the admission that your problem has been the drug. So whatever justice you think is being rendered in the institution, or whatever injustices we believe entitled us to the grievance that necessitated us altering our consciousness, using the drug, we're not concerned about.

We do know this: If you don't use the drug, things will get one hell of a lot better than they are. And that by continuing that practice of sharing the common problem, the solution will be obvious to you. Okay?

We'll finish *How It Works*. 11 and 12 I'm going to read to you because this is how we changed our life. Listen. *...sought through prayer and meditation to improve our conscious contact with God <u>as we understood Him</u>, praying only for knowledge of His will for us and the power to carry that out*. The idea of God dependency that I am offering you will be a discovery of a Power that you never dreamed of. And your capacity of not defending yourself from this world that seems to be attacking you, based on the power of the growing certainty of your innate sensibility that many of us in this room share.

What we're saying is, if on a day-by-day basis you don't have to sedate yourself; you can do anything in the universe. Can you hear that? The recovery that you experience through the power of God will open doors and make available to you dreams of careers, plans that you made that were dashed by the simple inability of being unable to perform them, always based on the excuses that you used to keep yourself in a condition of the gratification of your need for the drug.

So everyone in this room…. On this video, there's going to be a little place where the counselors if they want to, where those of you who are gathering to share this solution, to write to us. We will have available ex-cons, which we all are. Are you all ex-cons? All of us are basically ex-cons. We were locked in that vicious cycle of the drug. I promise you we'll be available to you, and we'll offer you the love that we want you to accept from us in our certainty that through our love by the solution of the problem we need to help you in order to work our programs.

Can you understand that? We want to help you, because the more we can serve and give, the more certain we can be that we are rendering a service that will help us realize a continuation of the discovery that we have made.

Number 12. *Having had a spiritual awakening as a result of these steps, we tried to carry this message to alcoholics and to practice these principles in all our affairs.* I don't know what a spiritual awakening is, but everyone that I know who is happy without the need to drug will connect it to a spiritual experience. I don't know what it means to be able to "white-knuckle it out." I don't know what it means to say, "I'm determined not to drink, and I'm going to use the power of my own mind not to do it," first of all, because I couldn't do it, and second, had I been able to do it, I would have remained unhappy for the rest of my life, because I was being denied what I had to have to have my enjoyment.

So what was required of me is that I change my mind about what I really wanted to be. Is this all right? [Yes] It's so fundamental sometimes, I forget what we're actually sharing here. Out there? I don't know what you think of this old guy, sitting here, but I've been doing this a very long time, and I want to show you that sitting next to you is very likely somebody that's going to say, "Why don't we give this a try?"

Look at it as a workshop. Look at it, out there, as an idea of something that you can practice while you're in there. Will you be tested by it when you come out? Of course. Of course. You're going to be tested immediately by it. But the support when you come out will be there, won't it? [Yes] We're going to help them.

Most of the programs that I am speaking of are already in place. But the point of the association of the drug with incarceration has become so big that it needs to be addressed. Is this so? [Yes] So you there? You tell the warden you want to start a program of Alcoholics Anonymous. You want to meet with those that share the problem. And if he tells you you don't need the program because you're going to be there for five years, you tell him to call me. There's going to be a number. You listen to me. There's going to be a number that appears on the board. All he wants to assure is that you're going to end up back in prison again. He doesn't want to have to deal... He knows that when you go out there, you're going to have to finally face the same problem that's going to bring you right back to him.

I don't know how prevalent that is with institutions. I doubt that it's prevalent. I guess to a human it might make sense, "Why do you need the program when you can't drink, anyway?" All that means is that as soon as you get out, you'll go back to what you were doing. We want to change your mind now. And we will. All right?

Many of us exclaimed, "What an order! I can't go through with it." Don't be discouraged. No one here has ever been able remotely to make an entire application to this. We claim spiritual progress, not spiritual perfection. That means I knew this morning that I was not going to take a drug. I could make that decision today, and I knew it would work.

Tonight, when I go to bed, I'll say, "Thank You." And I'll say, "Thank You," because when, in my desperation, I asked for help, I got it and it was you. It wasn't some mysterious antidote that I could take. It wasn't some magic formula that was going to relieve my intense necessity to drug. It came about through sharing the single problem and the single solution. Thank you for listening to me.

Okay, we'll just finish the steps. *The point is, that we were willing to grow along spiritual lines. The principles we have set down are guides to progress. We claim spiritual progress rather than spiritual perfection. Our description of the alcoholic, the chapter to the agnostics,* whatever you thought God was doesn't concern us. ...made three things very clear: *[that we] were alcoholic and could not manage our own lives; that probably no human power could have relieved our alcoholism;* and *that God could and would if He were sought.*

Does it say, "found"? It says, "sought." It says, if you really want the solution and you seek it, the solution will be available to you.

And I want to thank you for listening to me on this video. The idea that you're being allowed to see it is an indication that somewhere, if you believe and share with us the idea of miracles, if you'll let this be a miracle for you at this time and in this place, it will open up a whole new door for you.

You trust us with this. We walked in your shoes, so whatever that means, we know what you're going through. We want to help. We have a program that has worked for millions of us, and it always hasn't worked out in front; it's worked by you forming a gang of those who have found the solution through coming together in the privacy. Most of us on the program consider ourselves to be a gang of some sort, and when you meet somebody else out in the world who you know has shared the solution to your problem, you smile and you nod at each other, with no need at all to acknowledge to the world the solution that you found. That's a gang. And it will give you a great deal of joy.

We'll have a little sign we'll design for you, which you can signal to the other guy. What is the one? What do we use? I've run into them in the time that I've been in, and I've run into them everywhere. I can sense by what they say a lot of times. Are you that way? [Yes]

Thank you for sharing this meeting with me and your tolerance for my need to present this particularly to those who are incarcerated. This is a program of recovery that has given us a great deal of new-found faith in what we have found.

I'm going to open up the camera for just a moment to anyone that would like to sit in this chair, who might have something to say to somebody that's in jail. How many of you have been in jail? Okay. How many knew what you were in jail for? Phew! How many in jail again! I don't want you to tell your story. But it would be kind of nice. Everybody's got three minutes. You come and sit, and you look at the camera, and you say, "Hey, you out there? I've been where you are. Come on out and share the solution that we found together." Okay? You want to do it? You're up. Three minutes!

Dwell not upon the past today. Keep a completely open mind, washed of all past ideas and clean of every concept you have made. You have forgiven the world today. You can look upon it now as if you never saw it before. You do not know yet what it looks like. You merely wait to have it shown to you. While you wait, repeat several times, slowly and in complete patience:

The light has come. I have forgiven the world.

Realize that your forgiveness entitles you to vision. Understand that the Holy Spirit never fails to give the gift of sight to the forgiving. Believe He will not fail you now. You have forgiven the world. He will be with you as you watch and wait. He will show you what true vision sees. It is His Will, and you have joined with Him. Wait patiently for Him. He will be there. The light has come. You have forgiven the world.

A Course In Miracles, Lesson 75

A Beginners
12-Step Meeting
The Message Tonight:
How It Works

Boy, oh, boy, you guys are back.

Good evening. My name is Chuck, Chuck.... I've been using my last name, anyway. My name is Chuck Anderson, and I'm an alcoholic.

[Hi, Chuck!]

Hi, everybody.

There's a certain.... Whew! Look at that one! Sometimes, you know, the stigma of an addiction.... Addictions are stigmas, guys, and while now we pretend that there's a counseling that goes on, the fact of the matter is that there's a certain ostracizing that goes on that's connected to alcoholism, like is connected to all drug things. Generally speaking, those of us of this nature get here only as a last resort. That's just the way that is. And it's not that way because I *say* it is. It's that way because that's my experience. Just as many of us share the experience of the fellowship of *Alcoholics Anonymous* with the certainty that, until we finally stood up.... And I don't know what you guys connect with "alcoholic." I have no idea. But there was no intention on my part, over a period of many, many years, that I was going to admit that I had lost control of my drinking. After all, I was extremely successful, apparently, in what I was doing. And there was no manner in which I was going to admit that I would actually stand in front of you now.

And I have a great deal of difficulty doing it now, because I can share with you the experience of many of us of the relief that we felt when we finally said it. You know, I mean, "My name is Chuck, and I'm a problem drinker." That's a joke. That's a joke, guys. "I mean, I have a little problem with alcohol, but I would never go so far as to say.... After all, I go to work almost every day and...." All the stuff, all the stuff that goes with our determination to continue, despite the certainty of the condition in which we find ourselves, to manage.

Say to me, "That's okay. I can manage." Say that to me.

[That's okay. I can manage]

Yes. Is this a closed meeting? Do you consider yourself...? We're not checking your credentials. I'm going to have to assume.... I think I will, since it's a beginners meeting, that all of you, while you may not be at your first meeting, are going to be willing to acknowledge that somewhere, perhaps, your life has become unmanageable. Otherwise, why are you at this meeting? That is not to say you're going to finally admit to me that it's totally unmanageable, but it does mean, perhaps, that you admit, "I'm having trouble."

So when you admit you're having trouble, one of your friends would say, "Would you like to go to a meeting?" And you said, "I know what you're talking about, and I don't need a meeting. I'm going to be all right."

So we spend our lifetime, and lifetime after lifetime, in attempting to solve the problem that somewhere, deep within us, we know is not solvable. And I'm speaking from a deep experience as a recovered alcoholic that there was no manner, ever, ever, from the time I can remember, in all of my successes and failures, where I was not in a dependency on altering my consciousness through ethyl alcohol. None.

I don't know how many of you share that, and I'm not concerned. Those of you who have formulated addictions to other substances are very willing to share with me the dependency that started to grow in you, even though your manageability still apparently was available while inside you were falling apart. Over a period of some years now on the Program, I have observed every possible idea in which you, as an addict, have attempted to solve a problem that finally is going to have to be admitted is not solvable.

And where you want to take that in your minds does not concern me, because tonight what I am going to offer you is not only a solution that I found to my addiction, but that a solution, through a spiritual encounter, further enhanced by my capacity and need to give it away, brought me to a point in my life where I realized that there was more to me than I had pretended, or the world had told me, through a continuing transformation of my mind, and that further, once the program that I had gone onto in Alcoholics Anonymous began to be applied to my daily life, I began to have experiences of a continuing contact with an Authority of power that transcended my mind. It's very important that you remember this.

And for those of you who don't know this, Alcoholics Anonymous is purely, purely and absolutely, a spiritual program of recovery from addiction. It has exactly nothing…. There's nothing in this, nothing — *nothing*…. Listen to me. There's nothing in here about counseling. There's not a single word in anything, thankfully for me. Had it been about counseling when I came around, I'd have laughed. There's no way you're going to counsel me to sobriety. It's just absurd. I would listen to you only to the point that I needed a drink.

One of the reasons why the decision from a very, very old.... I wonder if I should talk about that. There's a very, very old Oxford Group that were the initiators of the possibility of a spiritual contact with God that finally became the 12-Step Program. Most of you know that. It's a program where businessmen, or affluent men, would gather together to express problems that were unsolvable in their life and became solvable by shared prayers.

The fundamental nature of the 12-Step Program is *literally* — is literally — "I can't solve the problem. He will if I let Him." There's nothing else in the Program. And those of you who say "I know all about the 12-Step Program" are, I'm sorry to tell you, dead wrong. You *do not know* about this program. If you knew about this program, your problems would be over forever. You would walk around each day, saying, "I'm happy. I have found a contact with God. When I got up this morning, I saw that today, well-lived, was going to afford me everything I could ever ask. From that moment on, this program began to give me happiness. And while I suffered in a condition of a reassortment of my life, my inability to perform particular functions, perhaps, that I did, it was nothing compared to the relief...." This is the *Course in Miracles*, incidentally. It's nothing that I could compare with the relief that I found in the security that evolved in me over my realization that I had really one single problem and that I had found the solution. So I didn't have to bury my addiction into all sorts of complaints about other problems that I had. The simple fact of the matter is this teaching, fortunately for us in a spiritual content, says literally, "I have one problem and one solution."

I had a great sponsor, and he would always.... His name was Roy Blankenheim. And all he would say to me every time I brought it up, he'd say, "You've got one problem: it's booze. You've got one solution: don't drink!"

When you've drunk successfully — do you hear that? — over a period of many years, and I had drunk successfully.... Obviously, I was successful. And I drank before my successes and I drank after them. And, of course, I drank in my failures, because after all, I was entitled to some solace. Ha! So pretty much, alcoholics or many of you who have other drug addictions will always use justification in your association for performing the drug, and the frigging truth (pardon me), the truth of the matter is it doesn't have anything to do with your situation. If you can't find a situation, you'll invent one so you can shoot up or smoke or do something, anything to relieve the tension of the necessity for a fix, based on your inability or fear to deal with the world. Say, "Of course." [Of course] That's for you guys who are sharing this with me.

And that's an intense fear that will grow in us. And the more it grows, the more we hide it. What we are representing is the natural human condition. And I know this may seem strange to you, but the question has always arisen in the Program whether alcoholism is hereditary. And I have no answer to that. My father happened to be one, and my brother's one, and my sister's one. And my grandfather was one, and his father was one, and my mother is one. And we also had a big business, and of course.... But we were all.... They call us "Scotch drunks." The Andersons were.... Yes.

So it sort of, I think, built to some sort of a climax in me. The relief that I experienced with the drug ethyl alcohol is the relief that the species *homo sapiens* has shared since the discovery of fermented mare's milk. Alcohol, C_2H_5OH — ethyl alcohol is what it is — will give a hell of a lot of relief to you because it gives you relief. It's something that's been missing in your system. Do you understand?

So it was very obvious to me the first time I took a drink.... I can remember. I must have been in the eighth grade. I don't know. I took a drink of wine in the alley and went like this, "Oh!" And it was like, "Ah ha!" And I'm talking to some of you here. It was just like, "Ohhhh! Yeah! *That's* how everybody deals with this."

Now, for those of you who express this in different ways or those of you, perhaps, who had, from the beginning, been able to deal with your problems within the range that they were expressed, bless you. The admission that I could not deal with the problems of my mental condition from the beginning were my acknowledgment, as many of our alkie friends share, that our minds often appear to operate under different procedures than so-called "Normalsville." We used to say.... Remember? I always used the term "normal." You'd say, "Well, you're not normal." "Well, I don't know whether I'm normal." We always say, Normal's a town in central Illinois. But I know that I wasn't normal.

And it was difficult for me to see that in fact, the ratio of the correlation of my conceptual mind in solving problems was different than the average human being. In case you'd like to know it, those of you who know what I am now, it's fundamentally the same principle of problem/solution that I employ in my enlightenment. I underwent an experience, as Bill Wilson did, and I was enlightened, as Bill was.

The founder of the 12-Step Program, Bill Wilson, underwent an illuminate experience. How many of you are aware of that? Most of you are. The founder Bill Wilson, who founded the *Course*.... I keep trying to connect him with the *Course*. See, for me the AA Program is *A Course in Miracles*. I'm very much aware that it was a miracle. I'm very much aware that there's no way, there was no power on earth that was going to stop me from drinking. Are you comfortable with that? And you can say, "Oh, gut it out! Sure, there is. Get a hold of yourself." All the stuff.... You know. It's just stuff. "What's the matter with you? Why can't you be like other people?" Shall I tell you? You aren't like other people.

I've been around for quite a while, and every time I discover somebody who had been unmanageable and finds the solution, I find that I share a lot of common characteristics with him in the manner in which I solve problems, often obtusely. I ran some companies. My ability to solve a problem was connected to my ability to step back from the problem and see various ways to solve it. That's generally considered to be an alcoholic mind. The more capacity you have to look at things — we used to call it "creative mind" — the more, eventually, you may need to sedate yourself, simply because you have so many solutions that.... Can you hear this? Is this all right? Do you mind me telling you this?

On the Program we used to call it "mind speed." We had another word called "mind-f'ing." I won't use the word, but you guys use the F-word all the time. But for us, you'd say, "Geez, I'm just mind-f'ing! Every time I get a hold of something, I just chew it. I can't let it go. It turns into a resentment, incidentally, and I'll never let the resentment go. And it builds up in me perhaps over a conceived wrong." "Somebody cut me off." You could get cut off. Anything could happen to you, and you could *build* it up in your mind. And that was true of the things that you loved and wanted, and the things that you wanted to serve and the joy that you wanted to have at Christmas, and the way that you went to church on Sunday. It simply involved everything that you did, because somehow you wanted to live life, and your life would become so full that initially you needed it to sedate your mind. Many of our alkies needed it just to get us calmed down. Now, that obviously became a necessity for us to continue to drink.

Without getting into my story, over a period of years it obviously became worse and worse, and generally, there's a point for many of us, hidden drinkers, like.... Let's just say that I was drinking a quart of vodka a day for ten years. So I was very well able to deal with alcohol and still function. I think it got.... Maybe it was only a fifth a day. And I always thought nobody could smell vodka on me, anyway. Right! At eight o'clock in the morning.

So I'm going to share something with you just because I feel like it. I was with a major music company. I had gone out of broadcasting. I was in broadcasting. I was a newsman when Kennedy was assassinated, and I was simply unable to deal with that, so I'd gone with a major music company, and I obviously had an alcohol problem. And I'm what you call a success.... I was able to function with alcohol. It's a little bit like they complained that Grant was drinking too much, and Lincoln says.... I always used to use that one. "General Grant is drinking a quart of booze a day." And Lincoln said, "I wish you'd give my generals whatever it is that Grant's drinking." And somehow that was one of my classic alcoholic defenses.

What began to happen there was I was performing, and somehow that will happen in major corporations. They just promote you to another job. I don't know if you've ever seen this happen, but: "Well, he's drinking a lot." "That's all right. Get him up here. Use his ideas." And it happened to me. So I ended up as sales manager, and they moved me to Chicago. And I was in a hopeless condition. And everybody *knew* it. Somewhere along the line we finally aren't hiding ourselves from ourselves. The collapse usually includes waking up in jail and not being certain why you're there.

I mean, it's one thing to wake up in jail and, you know, know that you've been arrested because you were.... You know. And you say, "Oh, shit. I got a ticket." It's another thing to wake up in jail with a bump in your head and have absolutely no idea how you got in jail. And I won't go into that story, but there were a couple of incidences where I was being reminded that I was unmanageable. And the time came.

I knew all about Alcoholics Anonymous. My goodness' sake! I knew probably more about Alcoholics Anonymous than most of the guys who were in the program. The first time I tried it, I was drunk, of course. First meeting that I went to....

You know, I'm a little confused by what goes on these days. Now they have alkie treatment centers, where they're going to send a guy for thirty days to detox him so they can gradually bring him down somehow so he never faces, really, the outcome of his drink. And I'm not criticizing it. We used to bring a guy down with a shot of Granddad when he started into the DT's. So I've been around a while.

But drunks were allowed to go to AA meetings. I don't know if they are today, but he came there because he was a drunk. What are you going to do? Kick him out because he's drunk and can't...? "You can't come to an AA meeting because you're drunk. Go to a rehab center and get yourself counseled dry, and they'll make you go in order to qualify for payments." And that's okay. I'm not being critical of it. But that's not how it works. At least, it didn't work for me that way.

So I explained to everybody, drunk at the meeting, all about the Program, and I had alkies that just looked at me, fortunately, guys that looked at me and smiled and said, "Yeah. Keep coming back. Yeah. You'll be all right." Oh, beautiful! Isn't it? "There but for the grace of God...."

And somewhere along the line I discovered a quality of understanding that I had never experienced. And I'm going to just lay this on the line for you. Regardless of what other meetings I have been to, and I was a meeting guy.... I've been to every kind of meeting there ever was, from the Kiwanis Club to you name it. So I suddenly came into a meeting where I could sense a communication that transcended the problem that was being expressed, as though, when they walk into the room, they come into the room to say, "I have solved the problem." I know that, apparently, has been reduced to coming into the room and sharing the retention of the problem.

The AA Program that I know — many, I'm sure, are still there — the AA meetings were gatherings where we came together to share the solution. Raise your hand if you don't hear that. And I'm sure you don't hear that. You don't. In other words, it's not a counseling session. I watched a TV program. It was absurd. They were all — what? Losers. They came together (and every single one of them was forced to go to meetings by their counselor) and said, "Wow! Those were the days. I can't do that anymore." And all they told was their story of defeat.

The basic meaning of an AA Program is to come and say, "I found the solution to my problem. I've got to go to meetings in order to keep it," so that everybody that came into *any* meeting came there with the certainty that on a day-by-day basis he had solved his problem. Is that clear to everybody? And they would pick me up and take me to meetings.

Now, whatever they had, suddenly I wanted it, because I could listen to their stories.... It isn't that they didn't tell "first-step stories," they're called. They did. They'd say, "I did this. I did that." I saw that there were some were worse or some were better, but every single one of them expressed — say to me, "common solution." [Common solution] Yes! Everyone that I looked at, who I began to measure against what I knew had to happen to me, was expressing a spiritual realization that relieved them from the necessity to continue the addiction. It might include all the other things that go with that, but that was basically it.

It included things like "Enough is enough," "I can't do it," "I need help." All of those things were a part of it. But the fact of the matter is, when I went to that meeting and saw that I was not drinking and they told me, "That's the way it will work for you if tomorrow you will say, 'I'm not going to drink today....'" The idea of "one day at a time" had never occurred to me. As much as I enjoyed living, my living was based, always, on a particular association with the advantage that I have gained in order to enjoy one day at a time, which is not exactly "one day at a time." It's more like a workaholic or something. Yes.

So whatever it was, I can remember. This was a beginners meeting. And I can feel it in *Course in Miracles* groups, and I can feel it in quiet times. And I would walk into the Monday night Wheaton beginners group, and I would come in, and I would begin to feel it almost immediately. I could feel a relief at being there. I hope that when you come here tonight that you can begin to feel a relief at the spiritual message that I want to give you in solving my problem. I want you to feel that when you see "I'm not like that anymore. I'm coming here," and then all of the axioms like "Take it easy," "One day at a time," "I've got to give it away to keep it," "Keep it simple, stupid!" "Easy does it...." I know them all, because that's how it worked. I didn't have to believe them; I just had to say it.

See, the Workbook.... I've got to go to the *Course in Miracles.* The Workbook says, to contact God all you have to do is say it. I mean, the idea that "I'm an...." The first time I said, "an alcoholic," I didn't know I was, but as soon as I said it, I began to say, "What a relief!" And that's called "working the program." And that means that on a day-by-day basis, whether you think it's going to work or not is absolutely not important. The solution, or proof of it, is on that day you did not do what had made you unmanageable. And the less that you did it, the more happy you became over your new-found manageability. And as long as you didn't claim in any way that you were responsible for your new-found manageability, it worked.

Generally speaking, generally, if you began to take credit for the solution that you had found, you would fall on your ass. I'm sorry, guys, but that's the way it works. Can you get this? "Oh, well, I had a lot to do with my sobriety. See? I'm able to decide whether I can drink or not." As soon as I thought I could decide whether I could drink or not, I would take a drink to prove how valuable my decision was, having forgotten entirely that the decision to drink was a part of my.... Say to me, "cunning and baffling." [Cunning and baffling]

I don't know how many stories.... (My socks are coming off.) I don't know how many stories you'd like to hear, but I have seen things happen that would prove alcohol is cunning and baffling. I'm going to tell you one. There's a guy named

Clyde.... What was his last name? No, his name was Wayne or something. Anyway, I knew him. I was his sponsor. And he had a big real estate office, a group of offices. And he was great. He worked the program. He went to a lot of meetings, and he really had a.... And he had a year. He had a year, and he was coming up to his first anniversary. So he said, "I would like to talk open at Naperville." Naperville is a suburb, and it's a big, open Saturday night, where there might be two hundred people there. And he was determined to talk open after a year. And a strange thing happened to him. He got a little nervous, so he decided to have a couple of belts. He decided to have a couple of belts so that he would be able to be relaxed in order to give his talk on being an alcoholic.

I don't know if that seems strange to you. Perhaps you'll say to me, "Well, that doesn't make any sense." That's what we mean by "cunning and baffling." It's cunning because it's in there, yet when he took the drinks, it seemed perfectly rational that it would be okay for him to just have those two. And the reason it got a little embarrassing, because if you haven't had drink for a year.... They always say, when you slip, you go right back to where you would have been, had you been drinking for the whole year. And it got just a little bit strange. He's standing up there, and it became obvious, almost immediately: "Oh, God!" He was around for a couple of decades since then. He's a lovely guy. That's really all he needed.

But I just wanted to show you the idea of "cunning and baffling." It always seems to be.... All addicts are that way. "Just one more time." Or "This time it will be okay. What happened to me before won't. I'll take more precaution. I'll hide my own car keys. I won't remember where I put them." All sorts of stuff. Come on! I don't know where you guys are with this. "If I can just get one more, I'll be okay." Yes, that sort of thing, which are indications of your addiction.

I had a guy, Dave O'Brien, who never made it. He was okay. He was a contractor, and he was okay, but his *truck* would turn into the bar. That's called "a classic slip." Now, after so many years, he would be thinking about something, and he'd turn into the bar. And I'd say to him.... I'd go and bail him out or whatever. I'd say, "Dave!" He says, "I don't know how I got there! I was driving along, and my truck made the turn." And he ended up in a head-on, and I remember.... Yeah. He didn't hurt anybody else, thankfully. And I went to his wake, Irish wake. And he was lying there, and I was looking at him, and all of a sudden, he was standing next to me. I mean, *literally* standing next to me. And it was something like this. A great Irish guy. We used to call it "the Irish disease." And he said to me, "How do I look?" And I said, "Dave, you look great." And all his alkie buddies were there.

This is a guy that struggled, maybe, for five or six years. And he would just keep coming back. And he would just keep coming back. And he just couldn't get it. And he got it. It was okay. When he stood there, I said to him, "It's okay." So I walked over to his mother, or one of the other alkies did, and he said, "Too bad that he couldn't have continued to go to AA meetings." And she said, "Oh, he was never *that* bad. Oh, no, my son was never bad. He didn't have to go to meetings." He was lying in the casket. Bless her heart. I gave her a kiss and said, "Good." But somehow, what we were sharing at that wake was our certainty that "There but for the grace of God go I." And we would suddenly remember all the times that we had no business doing what we did and how that had come about.

So that's a little sharing of my story. Once I discovered that through this spiritual contact on a continuing basis, that I didn't have to consume ethyl alcohol, it began to spread in me in other directions. Almost immediately I had to give it away, because I am a communicator, anyway. That's what I do. And I began to assume 11 and 12-Step Programs, those of you who aren't familiar, made 12-Step calls. And over a period of a few years I became very closely identified with what we call "Anonymous Anonymous." And I don't know whether that means anything to you, but there are a lot of us who couldn't go to public Anonymous meetings. Are you familiar with home groups?

There isn't any secret about this. A home group is composed of someone who, out in public, cannot even be seen as a recovered alcoholic. And there are a lot of them. And over a period of that three years, they would come to my house, and there would be maybe fifteen or twenty of them. And we had everything from judges to doctors to lawyers. We even had an Indian chief. We *did*, too. But, I mean, these are the guys. These are the guys that are running the community. I guarantee you this is true.

And, of course, I was able to share some stories that gave me a little more insight.... In fact, it had to do with my awakening. It gave me an insight into the fallibility of those who run our system. It allowed a physician to say to me, "I killed.... I did that." Dr. Bob used to do that. "I know I made a mistake and that that patient is dead." Or a lawyer who couldn't represent his client. Or a judge.... Just all that kind of stuff. And while they wouldn't talk about it specifically, there were times, if I took a Fifth Step with them, where I would.... You know, that's the step where you confess to yourself, to God and to another human being the exact nature of your difficulties. So there's an advantage to that. It's not like a priest, because you don't have to give him absolution. All you have to do is listen to it. Are you all with me on what this program is? They are *relieved* of it simply by the expression of it.

It's very much like the Amends Step. The Amends Step is "Seek amends and make the amends." There is absolutely no requirement that the amend be accepted. I'm sorry but there isn't. If you want to hold the grievance of your amend not being accepted, you go ahead, but it's liable to get you drunk, because you'll use it as justification of not being understood. Don't ask for justice; ask for mercy. It sounds like one of my talks. "Well, I'm sorry I did that, dear, and I want to ask your forgiveness because I know that I shouldn't have done it and everything about it...." "I'll never forgive you!" What are you going to do? Get drunk?

If I can show you that in the action of forgiveness, you can relieve yourself of the burden.... Otherwise, there's no way that you won't begin to carry that resentment around. And while it might not get you drunk that day, resentment is what gets you drunk, anyway. The whole condition of the human being in its inability to deal with its mortalism, what we call "mortalholics...." When I look at you.... I consider humans to be mortalholics. Do you know what I mean? You're addicted to death. Everything that you do is a form of addiction. And when I look at the resentments that are inherent in you in the defense of your addiction, I'm surprised that you don't see it. This is *A Course in Miracles*. There's in you that need to defend your position, which is a form of resentment, because you know somewhere that your position is not defendable. Yet you don't know what else to do within your own mind.

Is this going anywhere? Are you all right with me here? It's hard for me to tell. I'm so much a part of this that when I go to the necessity for the simplicity of the Program — and many of you are aware, say, of the reporter yesterday — I am immediately aware of his inability to understand that my solution was spiritual. No matter what he may say about it, he cannot understand it. And that's kind of like what I talked about this morning. I'm able to share with you, in sympathy and empathy, my certainty that I know you're more unmanageable than you're admitting to me. I don't require that you admit it, but I would suggest that you look at your problem so at least you can admit initially to yourself that the problem is not solvable, and you will begin to share with me the experience of my illumination that shows you it's solved not by the means that you were employing. Say, "Of course." [Of course] Or don't say, "Of course."

So basically, the Program says, or the 12-Step Program says, there's no way you can solve the problem. No matter what you do, it's not solvable. And you say.... Say to me, "Yes, it is." Well, then try to solve it. What will happen to you? You'll solve it till you're dead. Cirrhosis of the liver didn't solve my problem. I just waited till my stomach went down and started to drink again. "Oh, you didn't have cirrhosis." The hell I didn't! So it's not solvable in that way.

So how does it work? Here's how it works. Everybody got a copy of this? Did we all get a copy of this? Oh, good! I'm glad the instructions were followed. "Situation as usual," as they say. The only thing I'm going to point out about this, and here's the 12-Step Program.... Some of you may not really have ever been to an AA meeting. I would admonish you, this is a closed meeting, and I would appreciate it if you recognize somebody here you know, that you don't go out and blab to the neighborhood that you saw him. Okay, what you see here, leave it and go out into the world. I think that would be a good thing to do, because what you're sharing may not be understood by the world. But the relief that you may experience in being allowed to admit that you can't solve the problem may be very valuable to you.

Okay. Two things about *how it works*. This is from the Big Book of *A Course in Miracles*. It's past tense. [*A Course in Miracles*] Oh, shut up! I'm going to employ my technique that you guys know about. When I stand up to give a talk.... I used to do a lot of speaking, and you know, I've got it written right up here. What does it say? "Help!" On the other side it says, "Thank you." You think I'm kidding? There it is: "Help!" So if I begin to.... "HELP!"

Did it solve your problem? I don't know. Thank you. It gave me a little chance to look more at what I'm doing. It was an admission at that moment that I couldn't solve it. And I discovered that in a constant spiritual contact the solution was immediately available to me. Interestingly enough, it soon was not connected to drinking. You could connect the solution to anything — isn't it? Anything that was happening to you, I discovered that the spiritual solution would work in all circumstances. And this is all Big Book, and this is what it says here. And it literally changed my life. And the illumination that ensued after my years of service had to do with an assumed responsibility of communication that I can only attest to the Will of God. This turned into Jesus Christ, but my connections on the 12-Step Program are not with Jesus Christ, because he's inevitably misunderstood within the framework of what we do.

I mean, you can have Jesus Christ as your personal savior and be drunk every day of your life or kill or hurt. This is a program of self-realization that is espoused by Jesus Christ, who says, "Turn your will and your life over to God. I am your solution." Some of us would have a tendency to, for example, make our sponsor our solution. Some of you guys try to do that with me, perhaps. It's a very dangerous thing to do, because, for all you know, I'll be drunk tomorrow. Can you hear this? And if you use your sponsor as an idol — many of you know this — of how you're going to go, "After all, I'm following your program...." You work your own program, because no matter how he appears to be to you, he's only a drink away, just like you.

"Who has the most seniority," we used to say, "was the guy that got up earliest this morning." I mean, I've heard all sorts. I've been around for a few twenty-four hours. There isn't any secret to my.... Not me in '73. I don't know. You can add that up, but I struggled a little bit in.... What year is this? ['99] '99?! '72, '82.... I've been around a lot. But I've never stopped applying "a day at a time," because it becomes a natural thing for us to do. And the spiritualness of me began to grow. And it disrupted my life a little bit, but not a lot. I opened a rehab center. I did. I solved it by helping out. I was going to do that and all the things that went with that. But it continued, and suddenly I began to have experiences of all the things that went with what I teach you about what happened to me. I would call your attention to: my subsequent illumination had nothing to do with doctrine whatsoever. It had nothing to do with Jesus Christ or *sat-chit-ananda* or *kundalini*. It had nothing to do with a spiritual path, except the path of turning my will over to God and service. Always only give it away to keep it. And suddenly it began to work me.

Those of you who know me and wonder "who the hell that guy is" have never, ever, ever heard me say that I solved this problem myself. And all the directives I'm going to get from the press, who say they are following your instructions, are simply full of crap. There's no way that I can direct my attention to what you are within your own mind. The guy yesterday said to me, "How am I doing?" It's like asking an alkie saying to me, "How am I doing?" I said, "I don't know. How is it with you today?" I said, "Why are you asking me how you're doing? I don't know. This is a program of self-association and recovery." Somehow he considered me to be some sort of teacher that structured your life so that the solution…. That's absurd. There's absolutely no way that I can…. Never mind taking your inventory; I don't know your inventory. I have enough problems with what's occurring with me.

And I know you ask assistance from me in the direction of what you think I am, and I want you to understand, I'm offering you my assistance based on my certainty of what we are together. That's all. It has nothing to do with my inventory, what happened to me, the things I did. In many cases they may not even compare with what you have been able to tolerate in your own mind. I would only suggest to you that the pain in you — I'll use you — the pain in you that you are now controlling, it is not necessary that you have that. That's just the way it is. It's not that way because I say it; it's only that way because the tension that you consider necessary in order to justify your addiction to death is not true. Is that all right? There's no need for you to suffer the tension of a human condition.

Boy, there's a lot of light in here, guys.

So this is past tense. When you begin to read this, it will be past tense. It will be something that has already happened to you. *Rarely have we seen a person fail who has thoroughly followed our path.* And I don't know what *thoroughly* means, but I know the attempt to be thorough is better than not. *Rarely have we seen* him fail. It was originally written as "Never will we see him fail if he thoroughly follows it," but there's no way we could measure what "thoroughly" was. So it says, *Rarely have we seen a person fail. Those who do not recover are people who cannot or will not completely give themselves to this simple program.* Because it's very simple. It simply says, "Today, well-lived, will solve my problem. Today I don't have to do what I did." That's very simple.

But you must give yourself to the program, rather than requesting that the program give you the relief, because it can't. The relief is the surety that you involve in working that program. Nobody's going to measure your failure, and nobody will not tell you, on any program that I've ever been to, that "You can always do it again." This indicates that it has worked for you. "This is being offered to people. Perhaps it has worked." Later on, when I was still going to quite a few meetings, I remember they had begun a lot of counseling. And I was sitting in a beginners meeting. My home group was always a beginners meeting. It was always a Monday night beginners meeting. Always. In ten years, twenty years, I would go back to a beginners meeting.

And I was at a beginners meeting, and, you know, I came there because I wanted to. And there was some gal, Nancy or something. She said, "My name is Nancy A. and I'm a recovering alcoholic." And she had learned that, literally learned that in the treatment center. "It's an incurable disease. Therefore" — this is what they're still teaching — "you never can recover from it. So each day you have to be recovering." And later on in the meeting I said, "I need to have you explain to me what recovering has to do with this. This says that 'I have recovered.'" And now that's become a very dangerous word. That's nonsense.

If I got up this morning and am not going to drink today, I guarantee you I have recovered from alcohol. And for you to tell me I haven't, that I might drink tomorrow, means absolutely nothing to me. If I might drink tomorrow, it means that I'm still recovering. How can I have an experience of the relief of the necessity...? Excuse me. I didn't like it, because she could just continue to practice not drinking instead of saying, "No! I have found the solution. This is what I'm going to practice." So I was a little surprised by that. No, I am a recovered alcoholic. How long you have been recovered is not my concern. And for most of you, you hear that.

...usually men and women who are constitutionally incapable of being honest with themselves. Most alcoholics are not capable of being honest, but it's not constitutional. Somewhere they say, "I've had it." Constitutional incapability is what the death of a human being is. "No, it's not." Yes, it is. A human being is constitutionally incapable of simply admitting he can't solve the problem, and that's why he dies. Sorry, but that's the way it is. So you are constitutionally capable of choosing a decision of eternal life through God, regardless of what you tell me about your constitution, because obviously, if any constitution could do it, so can you. And that's just the way it works.

Now, did we cover one other situation? The word is "rigorous": *a manner of living which demands rigorous honesty.* That is, "I'm going to be honest with myself. I can't do this today. That's the program I'm going to follow." Some of you who are recently recovered from your addictions, I'd like to share with you that I'm not really that much an old-timer. There's no way that in any practice I have of what I am offering you I will not share the empathy of why you're in this room. This is the whole basis of my teaching. You cannot not be suffering from this condition, and there's no sense in trying to hide it from me. That's why you're here. You don't have to explain yourself to me. Nobody's going to check your credentials on whether you're a miracle worker or…. That's all in here, isn't it? Right there. Everybody? Put your finger there. You bet. That's one of our old practices. Never mind the other guy: "He did this and he did that." It's right here. Today, well-lived, will be that solution for you.

Their chances are less than average. There are those, too, who suffer from grave emotional and mental disorders. I used to meet a lot of them. *Many of them do recover if they have the capacity to be honest.* And we know that that's just an acknowledgment that there's no sense in trying to examine why somebody fails. They could fail for any and all reasons. Bill Wilson actually wrote the Steps in about twenty minutes. He just simply sat down and wrote them. And there were 12 of them. He had a lot of guidance going on in it, but this is the result of that.

Listen. *Our stories disclose in a general way what we used to be like, what happened, and what we are like now.* All spiritual programs, or descriptions of our shared relief, will describe to each other what we used to be like, what happened and how we are now. I used to wander through life, feeling pain and dying. I had an experience of awakening, and now I know that I am saved. Those are the three necessities, aren't they? 1, the acknowledgment of the problem; 2, the recognition of the solution; and 3, say, "Now." [Now] 3, how you are now. Not concerned with how you're going to be next week. It's simply not there.

But here's a crucial sentence in this, for those of you…. This is very true with *Course in Miracles* teachers, too. Listen. *If you have decided you want what we have and are willing to go to any* lengths *to get it—then you are ready to take certain steps.* If you have decided that you would like to share an immediate contact with God and are willing to go to any lengths.... The reason I say, "any lengths," is that at any moment a commitment is all the length that there is. In the Workbook of *A Course in Miracles*, Jesus says, if you will do that today, that will be all the length that there is. Those of you who heard Master Diana do the first eight steps of the Workbook are very much aware of that. Each one of them individually will be an indication of any length. Each one of them. *My meaningless thoughts are showing me a meaningless world.* The admission of that is the only length you'd ever have to go to.

So once you have resolved to do that, you are ready to take certain steps. It doesn't say you've taken them, but it says you are ready to do it. The basis of my offering to you is: be ready to do it, and don't measure your readiness. Can you hear that? You want the solution. Pursue the solution based on the *Course*, and it will work. It cannot not, because power is given unto you that the solution is there if you will depend on the power of God for the solution rather than yourself. Okay?

...you are ready to take certain steps. At some of these we balked. All of us. *We thought we could find an easier, softer way.* I'm sorry, but this program is uncompromising. I'm sorry, but it just is. "No, it isn't." Yes, it is. "No, it isn't." Yes, it is. There is no softer way than the admission you can't solve the problem but God will. It's impossible. It's just impossible. In the *Course in Miracles* you can't see two worlds. Salvation can be seen as no compromise. There is no compromise between eternal life and time. That's actually what this says. Is this all right? There is no compromise in this. But it's so altruistic and uncompromising. Yes! Why? I'm powerless. I know the admission that I am powerless may require something else, but if I don't have that, I have nothing.

I'll use the *Course in Miracles*. Did I get it right that time? Yes. The training of the *Course in Miracles* requires that you admit in any moment that you don't know who you are or what you're doing, and each time you do it, the problem will be solved by the Second and Third Step. I'm almost to the Steps here. Because the Second Step is going to say that you make a decision to do it and whatever. We'll get to it.

Oh, *we came to believe* first. Hold it. This is kind of nice. *At some of them we balked. We thought we could find an easier* and *softer way. But we could not.* Listen. *With all the earnestness at our command, we beg of you* — beg of you, entreat you — *to be fearless and thorough from the very start* — because *Some of us have tried to hold on to our old ideas, and the result was nil until we let go* completely. There's no such thing in a program of addiction as partial success. That's just the way it is. You can't be partially successful at not drinking. That's the same as saying, "I'm going to cut down." Can you see that? "Oh, I'm going to be okay this time. I'll hold myself to two drinks after dinner. Well, look how successful I was." In the meantime, you're walking around like this. The next thing you know, you're watching the clock for when you can have the next one. That's called "Look how successful I am at not drinking."

We used to called those, "white knucklers." Are you familiar with the term? Bob Smith, the other founder of the *Course in Miracles*, Dr. Bob, of the.... Oh, I.... The hell with you! You know, can I share something with you? Dr. Bob and Bill Wilson were the founders of the *Course in Miracles*. There. That took care of that. Now every time I do it, stop telling me it's not so. It's impossible that there was not divine intervention. A white knuckler is a guy who never gets it spiritually. No matter how hard he works, he must express his own determination not to drink. And he's much happier than he would have been, had he drunk. And this was Dr. Bob up until he died. What a great guy!

And that's fine with me. What is it that I am offering you? I can only offer you the solution that you're willing to accept. There's no criticism involved if you decide in the *Course in*

Miracles to work the program and can't get it. What do I care? You can't come around me and have it not work, because I am your guarantee that it worked. So Dr. Bob would come with Bill Wilson, and he said, "Boy, I'm glad you're here, because without you, there wouldn't be a program." Bill turned to him and said, "Dr. Bob, without you there wouldn't be a program, either." Can you see that? I need someone who expresses the discipline that's necessary in order that the solution can be found. This is a pretty good talk, if I ever get into it.

Wait a minute. . . . *the result was nil until we let go absolutely. Remember that we deal with alcohol.* It is *cunning, baffling and powerful! Without help it is too much for us. But there is One who has all power—that One is God. May you find Him now! That One is God. May you find Him now!* And I don't care how you hear that. And I don't care who you think God is. God will solve the problem if you let Him.

Half measures availed us nothing. We stood at the turning point. We ask *His protection and care with complete abandon.* That's the Workbook of *A Course in Miracles.* We stood at the turning point, trying to decide whether we should pursue this other course that we had. We knew that half measures were not going to avail us. We were going to be right back where we started. So we said very simply, "We ask for His care and protection with complete abandon."

I'm going to see how that sounds. Say to me, "complete abandon." [Complete abandon] "I would never completely abandon myself to something that I didn't know what it was." Then continue in your practice. The little prayer video that I did indicates that your contact with God comes from the abandonment of yourself. There's no possibility that you're going to perform any act within your own conception that's going to offer you the entirety of the solution. And say to me, "That's too simple." [That's too simple] "Explain to me what you mean by that." I mean complete abandon. "Yes, but what do you mean by 'complete abandon'?" I mean complete abandon. "How will I know if I've completely abandoned?" You'll feel the peace of God. "You didn't answer my question." Yes, I did.

That's exactly what I was doing with this guy yesterday. Wow. To him it seemed very ambivalent. What I say is: my problem was solved by my inability to solve it. He registers that as weakness or a power to attempt to find God, and not being able to do it is actually what our solution was.

Here are the steps we took, which are suggested as a program of recovery. [1.] *We admitted we were powerless over* _____ *and our lives* were *unmanageable.* Put in anything you want there. Say that to me, "I admit that I'm powerless over" — what? Anything. "And that my life is unmanageable." And it will work perfectly. "I can't do this. I don't know what the solution is, but I can't do this any more. I don't want to admit it to anybody because they'll discover how weak I am. They'll try to buck me up. They'll say, 'Why can't you be like the rest of us? Why are you acting the way you are? Brace up. You're weak.'" And all the other things that go with your fear of admitting that you are, indeed, powerless. At some point you've got to say, "Go to hell. I can't solve this problem," as much as your ego is going to come to you at that point and say, "Yes, you can. Here's another way for you to do it. Here's another way that you can stretch out your addiction. You're going to die, anyway," and all the other reasons that you'll get that are the cunning and baffling reasons why you refuse to abandon your life to the eternal life of God.

...we were powerless and *our lives had become unmanageable. Number 2. Came to believe that a Power greater than ourselves could restore us to sanity* is a sentence virtually out of *A Course in Miracles*. The restoration of your sanity is what the *Course in Miracles* teaches. I went to a lot of meetings over a lot of periods of years where guys said, "What do you mean, 'insane'?" You know: "Well, I wasn't really as insane as other guys." I'm not concerned about that.

This says, "will restore you to sanity." When I was asked to explain it, I said, "I don't know whether I was insane, but I sure as hell knew I did a lot of insane things. I beat my so-and-so, or I did that, or I abandoned...." All the things that go with that are obviously acts of insanity. And they are things that no one in their right mind would do. That's the requirement for that step. And we'd get the guy, wondering whether he's insane or what.... I just looked at him and said, "What are you doing here? Why don't you go out some more and find out whether you can be successful at this?" Wow.

[3.] *Made a decision to turn our will and our lives over to the care of God as we understood Him.* Is there a difference between will and life? Letting God's Will be done will be the relinquishment of your willful intent to assert that you can solve the problem. Your life will be included in that, because God's Will will show you a new life that will show you how happy you can be with the program. You will be made new by that. So that's our will and our life. Is there a difference between will and life? The Will of God is what your life is, and your acknowledgment of that will show you a new life.

So we're going to turn our will and our life over to God as we understand Him. And there's no requirement to understand Him at all. Many of the guys I know who have been around for a very long time would always say, "As I don't understand Him," would actually substitute that. "I'm going to turn my will and my life over to the care of God as I don't understand Him. My attempts to understand Him have gotten me drunk." No, quite literally. No. And they'd say to me, "I'm turning my will over to God as I don't understand Him."

You don't have to understand God in order to have His Will and life available. As a matter of fact, for most of us, our attempts to understand God was what the problem was, in trying to figure out why the hell He would be involved in all of this stuff. This says at the bottom, *Easy does it, First things first, Keep it simple, Live and let live, One day at a time,* and *Utilize, don't analyze.* Did I miss any? Those are the things that.... I better not tell them. There's an alkie back there who gave me all of those, and I don't know if I want to break his anonymity or not.

Look out! [4.] *Made a searching and fearless moral inventory of ourselves.* There are a lot of guys that are advised to actually write down what their problems are. And that's okay with me, but I want your problems to be inclusive. When you're dealing with the *Course in Miracles,* it will immediately tell you that you have one problem. That does not mean that if you have identified your problems as separate, they should not be included in the decision you have made to turn your will, because there's a tendency for you to leave something out. This is the basis of the Workbook. Leave nothing out in the new solution that you have found. That's how that works.

Stand by! [5.] *Admitted to God, to ourselves, and to another human being the exact nature of our wrongs.* It's very interesting that in the confession of sin, if that's what you want to call it, or the guilt that you feel, the necessity to admit it to God is pretty simple, because God is not going to respond. The next most difficult is admit it to yourself, because it's an admission that you actually have done the things that you've done. I don't care what they are. And admitting it to somebody else is the physical act of unburdening the necessity of defending your previous guilt.

I've taken a lot of them. And I haven't given absolution. Yet I've never seen a time when a guy got through with his 12th Step.... And I used to take.... He just got there, and we'd sit there and drink coffee, and I could *feel* the relief that he felt at God, himself and me. And we would sit there and he'd go something like, "Wow!" It didn't make any difference what it was; it was the *act* of giving it away where he found the solution. It didn't matter what the inventory was. I have listened to little, insignificant guilts that people have carried for years and years that really didn't mean a darn thing.

They're everything from stealing from Grandmother.... Just stuff. I've heard it, and I've listened to it, and they inevitably feel better for it.

Now, perhaps there's another step they may have to take after that is accomplished. Let's take a look. ...*the exact nature of our wrongs.* Now, there's a get-ready step that's put into here, so you don't go dashing out and try to make amends. Somewhere you're going to have to look at yourself and say, [6.] We *were entirely ready to have God remove all these defects of character.* It isn't that you tried to measure what you were going to do to solve it. All you had to do was make yourself ready for the solution. But notice that you're still going to have to make the amend. In a sense, making amend is asking for forgiveness. Do you understand that? All right.

Here's what it says. Then you [7.] make *a list of all persons* you have *harmed, and* become *willing to make amends to them all.* Notice it doesn't say that you have to make the amend. First you must become willing to do it. Forcing yourself to make an amend *will not work.* "I want you to call her right now and tell her, and, dog-gone, you're going to do it." That's not the way to do it. Sorry. Somewhere within you, you say, "That *was* wrong of me. I've done the inventory. I must be willing to do it, and if I'm not, I'm going to have to carry the pain around inside of me."

Now, we're going to look at the non-acceptability of the amend immediately, but.... Can I say something to you? And I've done a lot of work with this. In the vast majority of times, particularly with alcoholics, the idea that you would actually pick up the phone and make the amend, it works. It will work. And it will work sometimes in a very miraculous way. And those of you who have seen reconciliations based on this program.... It tears me up a little bit because I've *seen* this work. I've *been* with it when it worked. I've *been* with it when they say, "Boy, was I ever waiting for you to call!" I've *been* with it when they say, "I've been wanting to call you for all these years and let's do that." That, in the *Course*, is taught as forgiveness. Isn't it? "I'm sorry. Will you forgive me?"

Now, if it turns out with the world that they won't forgive you, that's okay, because the inventory that you're carrying is going to be your own, anyway. You cannot seek redress from a grievance and be successful on this program. It's not possible. Give it away, and it will work. Getting even will never solve your problem. And if there's one thing revengeful alkies know, it's that that is true, because some of that stuff you've been carrying around you've been carrying around since you can remember. And being able to reveal that you were molested and all the things that happened to you are very valuable to you. But if you intend to hold on to them and exercise the duress that you feel, what the hell good is it going to do you? Okay?

Say to me, "All pain is self-inflicted." [All pain is self-inflicted] You bet. Finally, it's not what he did to you. It's what you think he did to you and your inability to pardon him. It's going to be inside you, isn't it? And that's how that works.

[9.] *Made direct amends to such* persons *whenever possible, except when to do so would injure them* and *others.* And that's always put into there because there's a lot of people that don't want the wound brought up again, and to confess to something that they never knew about will just hurt them more. And how you do that in your own mind, I have no idea, but that's why that's in there. The idea that "Gee, I did do this. I'm really going to have to tell her. She doesn't know anything about it, but I...." You don't have to do that. I've given advice on this, too. But I know that will be all right.

Okay, here's an important step. This is the Workbook of *A Course*. [10.] *Continued to take personal inventory and when we were wrong promptly admitted it.* Okay? Do you hear me? "Don't let the sun set on a grievance" is the best advice that I can give you. Don't take it to bed. If you've got it, get rid of it. And this was one of the practices I did for a very long time. Do a little inventory at night and say to yourself, "How has it been for me today?" And don't try and measure it, because the acknowledgment of the wrong will be the absolution for it. Don't try to hide yourself from your program. I used to give talks on Number 10 that were very important because they're connected to 11, which is the basis of the teachings of a miracle course.

[11.] *Sought through prayer and meditation to improve our conscious contact with God as we understood Him, praying only for knowledge of His will for us and the power to carry that out.* That's the entire teaching: continued to request the solution, to know what His Will is, *and the power to carry it out.* What a lovely step!

Past tense: [12.] *Having had a spiritual awakening as a result of these steps... Having had a spiritual awakening as a result of these steps... Having had a spiritual awakening as a result of these steps....* What are we going to do? *...we tried to carry this message to alcoholics, and to practice these principles in all our affairs.* And this is all that has ever been asked of you or could be asked of you. I know this is going to say, *We claim spiritual progress, not spiritual perfection.* There is nowhere in the mind training that I am offering you that it's ever necessary for you to say, "I've solved the problem," only that "I've solved it at this moment, and I'm going to pursue in that direction, the solution." I think it will say that.

Many of us exclaimed, 'What an order! I can't go through with it." Do not be discouraged. No one among us has been able to maintain anything like perfect adherence to these principles. We are not saints. The point is, that we are willing to grow along spiritual lines. I know people that gave up the Workbook because they missed it for three days, and they said, "Hell, I can never come up. There's no sense in me doing any more." That's just the determination not to practice. Who are they kidding? At any single time.... Remember, in the Workbook of the *Course*, it's to bring about one change in you in which you can continue to practice. Solutions do not proceed in the way that they do in mind training. One solution of discovery of God will be all you'll ever have to have if you have admitted that you have one problem, because every time the solution is offered to you, you'll apply it to the solution that you found within your own life. Is that ever nice!

The principles we have set down are guides to progress. We claim spiritual progress rather than spiritual perfection. Our description of the alcoholic, the chapter to the agnostic, and our personal adventures before and after make clear three pertinent ideas: [(a)] That we were alcoholics and could not manage our own life. [(b)] That probably no human power could have relieved our alcoholism. and *[(c)] That God could and would if He were* — say, "sought." [Sought] *...that God could and would if He were sought.* Nowhere in this program does it say He has to be found. The seeking of God is what the finding of God is, and your definition of finding Him is what is losing Him. Christian? Is that all right with you? First seek God, and everything else will work, because you cannot not find Him if you seek Him. Knock and it will be opened unto you, and that's how simple this program is.

We're taking up more time, perhaps, than we should. For those of you who want to know, that's how it worked. And that's how it worked for me. And I was successful at it. And the manner in which I was successful at it was this: [The Twelve Steps]. It wasn't something else. It wasn't a particular counselor that helped me solve my problem. It was not that. You listening to me? You want to get a picture of this? I don't care. This was the solution to my problem, along maybe with this: [The Hazelden *Twenty-Four Hours a Day* book]. This is the last 150 lessons of the Workbook. Basically, it's the same.

I remember when, I don't know, some alkie told me this is not approved literature in the Alcoholics Anonymous. What kind of crap is that! "Well, it's too spiritual." You bet. This is the Hazelden Twenty-Four Hours a Day Book. It has one prayer for every day. It's very much like the *Course in Miracles.* Isn't it? So the discipline of it is to get up in the morning, sit down, read your Twenty-Four Hour Book, and let that be for the day. And I said, "You mean I have to do it every day?" And he said, "Yes, you have to do it every day." This is the *Course in Miracles.* "Well, I may miss a day." "No, you *have* to do it every day." "Well, what if I miss a day?" "How can you miss a day if you *have* to do it every day?"

No, this is actually what this says. And I discovered that once I decided to do it, it really didn't matter what it said. Can you hear that? It had to be a discipline of relaxing my mind, because here I'm in.... I can remember. I was in the real estate business by then, and I ran a couple of offices. And I was doing very well. And they're tooting the horn. And I run down. We're going out on a major inspection. I got into the car and was sitting, and I said, "Wait a minute!" I jumped out of the car. I ran up. I quick grabbed my Twenty-Four Hour Book, I sit down on the end of the bed, and I open it, and I read it.

I confess that sometimes I would read prayers that were not for that particular day. And after I had been around for a while, I was allowed to have favorite prayers, just as we're allowed in the *Course in Miracles* to have favorite lessons. So the ones I jotted down (and this will be the end of our lesson today), there's about three or four of them I'd like to read. The first one that I always did was June 1st. Yep. June 1st and 2nd. "Why did you always do June 1st and 2nd?" I like what it says. So here I am, and, you know, the idea that I was going to pray never really appealed to me, but I like what this says. Here's what it says. Ready?

You were born with a spark of the Divine within you. It had been all but smothered by the life you were living. That celestial fire has to be tended and fed so that it will grow eventually into a real desire to live the right way. By trying to do the will of God, you grow more and more in the new way of life. By thinking of God, praying to Him, and having communion with Him, you gradually grow more like Him. The way of your transformation from the material to the spiritual is the way of Divine Companionship.

That's the *Course in Miracles.* Isn't that nice? I like it. You grow more and more like God by praying to Him. And if that seems a little impossible, then how come it says that? How come Jesus said to me, "Therefore be ye perfect, even as your Father...."? But did it take practice? You bet. So then the next day, watch out! Oh, did I do June 2ⁿᵈ? Uh oh!

You cannot believe in God and keep your selfish ways. The old self shrivels up and dies, and upon the re-born soul God's image becomes stamped. This is kind of nice. It's kind of nice, isn't it? God's image becomes stamped. Is that ever lovely! *The gradual elimination of selfishness in the growth of love for God and your fellow human beings is the goal of life. At first you have only a faint likeness to the Divine, but the picture grows and takes on more and more of the likeness of God, until those who see you can see in you some of the power of God's grace at work in a human life.*

Isn't that lovely? That's a lovely prayer. And I would get up and say, "Wow! That's a lovely prayer!" The amazing thing is I really didn't have to particularly understand it, but somewhere it was beginning to work. Those of you who are working the *Course in Miracles* Workbook are beginning to shine and look real happy, very simply because this is how it works. And if they say to you now, "What's happened to you?" say, "I'm in a mind training program. I discovered the hell with it! There's an alternative to this." "Boy, do you look good! What is it?" That's what we want to happen to you. You are the demonstration that this works.

We have two more prayers and then we'll be through with this. For some reason or other, I picked out May 1st. Well, I'll do March 29th first. I don't know why. Because March 29th comes before May 1st. Initially, the reason I liked March 29th is I always liked the idea of wearing the world like a loose garment. One of the old traditions was to wear the world like a loose garment. Don't let the world cling to you. Do you hear that? So this is one of them, and I thought I'd read it to you.

I must live in the world and yet live apart with God. I can go forth from my secret times of communion with God to the work of the world. To get the spiritual strength I need, my inner life must be lived apart from the world. I must wear the world as a loose garment. Nothing in the world should seriously upset me, or can, as long as my inner life is lived with God. All successful living arises from inner life.

It's a nice book.

Our final one, then, will be one of my favorites. And it is May 1st. Are you ready? Oh, all right. May 1st:

All material things, the universe, the world, even our bodies, are only Eternal Thoughts expressed in time and space.

Oh, I see. I wonder where that came from. Once more:

All material things, the universe, the world, even our bodies, may be or are Eternal Thoughts expressed in time and space. The more the physicists and astronomers reduce matter, the more it becomes a mathematical formula, which is thought. In the final analysis, matter is thought. When Eternal Thought expresses itself within the framework of space and time, it becomes matter. Our thoughts, within the box of space and time, cannot know anything firsthand, except material things. But we can deduce that outside the box of space and time is Eternal Thought, which we can call God.

And that's my whole teaching to you. Okay?

Thank you for your patience in allowing me to express whatever it is that it was necessary for me to tell you in the connection with the solution that I found through the 12-Step Program. My necessity to do this has come about because, perhaps, it's necessary for a revival of the fundamental teaching that this is a *spiritual* program and that my sobriety and my serenity that I have found, my peace of God, is based on turning my will over to God, and not some sort of therapy, not some sort of direction of my ability to solve the problem. And that's why we did this lesson today.

And we're going to close it with the opening of the Twenty-Four-Hour book.

Look to this day, for it is life, the very life of life. In its brief course lies all of the realities, the verities of existence, the bliss of growth, the splendor of action and the glory of power. For yesterday is but a dream, and tomorrow is only a vision. But today, well-lived, makes every yesterday a dream of happiness and every tomorrow a vision of hope. Look well, therefore, to this day.

Thank you, Maggie. This is the end of our meeting. We generally say the "Our Father," if it's okay with you. Will you stand with me, please, and say the "Our Father"?

Our Father Who art in Heaven, Hallowed be Thy Name. Thy Kingdom come. Thy Will be done on earth, as it is in Heaven. Give us this day our daily bread. And forgive us our debts, as we forgive our debtors. And lead us not into temptation, but deliver us from evil: For Thine is the Kingdom, and the power, and the glory, for ever. Amen.

Keep coming back!

Father, our Name is Yours. In It we are united with all living things, and You Who are their one Creator. What we made and call by many different names is but a shadow we have tried to cast across Your Own Reality. And we are glad and thankful we were wrong. All our mistakes we give to You, that we may be absolved from all effects our errors seemed to have. And we accept the truth You give, in place of every one of them. Your Name is our salvation and escape from what we made. Your Name unites us in the oneness which is our inheritance and peace. Amen.

A Course In Miracles, Lesson 184

The 12-Step Program and A Course In Miracles: *Recovering From A Terminal Disease*

This is A Course In Miracles.

It is your path of enlightenment.

It is your journey without distance in the space of an instant of reality.

It is a required course. Only the time you take it is voluntary. Free will does not mean that you can establish the curriculum. It means only that you can elect what you want to take at a given time. The course does not aim at teaching the meaning of love, for that is beyond what can be taught. It does aim, however, at removing the blocks to the awareness of love's presence, which is your natural inheritance. The opposite of love is fear, but what is all-encompassing can have no opposite.

This course can therefore be summed up very simply in this way:

Nothing real can be threatened.
Nothing unreal exists.
Herein lies the peace of God.

MIRACLE MIND TRAINING

The purpose of the workbook is to train your mind in a systematic way to a different perception of everyone and everything in the world. The exercises are planned to help you generalize the lessons, so that you will understand that each of them is equally applicable to everyone and everything you see.

Transfer of training in true perception does not proceed as does transfer of the training of the world. If true perception has been achieved in connection with any person, situation or event, total transfer to everyone and everything is certain. On the other hand, one exception held apart from true perception makes its accomplishments anywhere impossible.

The only general rules to be observed throughout, then, are: First, that the exercises be practiced with great specificity, as will be indicated. This will help you to generalize the ideas involved to every situation in which you find yourself, and to everyone and everything in it. Second, be sure that you do not decide for yourself that there are some people, situations or things to which the ideas are inapplicable. This will interfere with transfer of training. The very nature of true perception is that it has no limits. It is the opposite of the way you see now.

MIRACLES

A miracle is a universal blessing from God through me to all my brothers. It is the privilege of the forgiven to forgive.

Miracles praise God through you. They praise Him by honoring His creations, affirming their perfection. They heal because they deny body-identification and affirm spirit-identification.

I inspire all miracles, which are really intercessions. They intercede for your holiness and make your perceptions holy. By placing you beyond the physical laws they raise you into the sphere of celestial order. In this order you are perfect.

- Jesus of Nazareth

We're glad that you decided to join us here in this time and place. All the particular references that you have given yourself in the purpose for being here we hope and trust that you'll be willing to lay aside for just a moment here in time. For this moment in time, if you can accept the fundamental premise of my offering to you, is the time and place where the entirety of the dilemma of your location in this place of sickness and loneliness and death was resolved.

All around the world now, through the auspices of the saviorship of Jesus Christ and his incredible Workbook of *A Course in Miracles*, the text of his declaration of your perfection is resounding with a very basic realization that the decision to be the manner in which I am observing you at this time and place was yours to make.

The reports concerning the healings that have been going on, among them, arthritis.... Remember how thousands of people around the world are reporting a relief in the laying down of the burden of the necessity to suffer from this condition?

Now, that was a review of an energy flow that brings a response to your idea of arthritis. Do you see that? Parkinson's Disease? Remember? Was it just yesterday or a hundred years ago that we offered you the certainty that in the time and place that you are in, you can recover from the dilemma of the dis-placement that has heretofore afforded you no relief for the manner in which you are constructed within the fearful idea of your self-identity?

So the healing videos, here they are. The moment of correspondence that offered you that relief from the necessity to suffer from anything is the purpose for this attraction. So if, for any reason, you believe that there is a reason other than the totality of your recovery from the sleep of death that you heretofore used to represent yourself as a belief for why you're here, I would ask that you just for a moment tolerate the totality of a realization of a methodology, the momentary study of a method, that continues to offer you a relief in the decision-making capacity.

There's no question that the power and light that is being provided to you at this moment will change your mind about your alternatives within time, your decision-making faculties, in a moment's realization that you are actually whole and perfect as you were created. The light, this light of healing, first will give you perhaps a great deal of peace, because you'll understand at this time and place that the entirety of the solution is available to you, not contained within the decision-making factors of your own mind, but in a sudden revelation of the light and love that's shining all around you.

Is it a miracle? Yes. Yes, you begin to see that light, don't you? You might want to say to me, "I think this is a miracle."

We like to look at the manner sometimes in which the miracle came about in our minds, and there's really no secret about the manner in which most of us came to know that the problem contained within ourselves in regard to the unmanageability that we were experiencing could not be solved out in this world. The basis of the teaching of Jesus Christ is that you will never be successful in solving the problem of the decision that you have made to remain in separation, and your necessity to call on a power, whatever it may be, greater than yourself, to solve it is the nature in which many of us came to know this.

Sometimes, when we begin to talk about recovery, we have a tendency to believe that "If we take this holy scripture, this scripture from the Savior Jesus Christ, who represents the Christian tradition in the manner in which together we can fight this battle and seek a solution, as he declares in the doctrine of his declaration that you can overcome the world, [that it] is a manner in which it was accomplished in many of us." Certainly, in my case that was not true.

My solution was not to thump the Bible. I'll try it if you want me to:

"Here is the living Son of God, giving you answers to all the problems that you could ever have!"

And I used to listen to that. And I'd say, "Which part of it gives me the answer? Which part of it is going to remind me that the solution lies in me, not out in the world? Which part of this scripture am I going to accept that indicates that Jesus Christ of Nazareth is in fact my savior?"

Certainly, the progress that I have made in regard to this idea of salvation based on the surrendering of my will has led me to the certainty that the scriptures of Jesus are to draw my direct attention, first of all, that I can't solve the problem that I feel in the pain and death of my human association and that he will be a provision, a spiritual provision within my heart and mind wherein the problem can be solved.

The solution that I am representing to you, as one of my determination as an addict to the need to sedate myself from the unsolvable problems of this world that I was experiencing, led me to a point in my mind where I saw there was no solution. I asked for help from whatever power might be.

There is always a certain curiosity about teaching to.... And I'm sure you're aware that we're speaking of the recovery of the 12-Step Program. We're speaking of the certainty that it's possible for you at a moment of totality of despondency to turn your will and your life over to the care of God. Yes.

The dilemma that you encounter in the idea of turning your will over to a power always involves the need for you to identify what the power is. We end up offering some sort of resolution to the problem by telling you, you're turning your life over to a power greater than yourself. Now, the attention that you don't turn your will and your life over to God are simply indications that the conceptual mind believes there are different gods or different kinds of gods and you fully intend to turn your will and your life over to a god that you can understand within the particulars of the irresolution you express in the pain that you identify as unsolvable.

The simple truth of the matter is: This entire offering to you is to turn your will and your life over to the inevitable conclusion of yourself in relationship with the addiction from which you previously suffered in your determination to somehow adjust to the incredible ideas of loneliness and pain that constitute this world.

Speaking to you directly at this time and place, I speak from the certainty of a spiritual experience that occurred at a point in my life where the problems of this world could not be solved. Now, the particulars in which I came to that realization and then went out and began to present it to the world are not really the manner in which it came about in me. The particulars of the demonstration of all of the, say, erratic behavior that occurred within my addictive nature were not what the solution was.

We're using the light and life of Jesus of Nazareth, and we were together this morning, talking about the particulars of a revolution that occurs in many of us somewhere in time, where we begin to act out determinations to free our self from the world. We can no longer tolerate the idea.... And I'm speaking to a lot of you out there now. Certainly it may include sedation, or the necessity to alter our consciousness sufficiently so we can find some relief from everything that's going on here.

If you wanted to compare it to Jesus of Nazareth, it would certainly help you to take the image that the world represents as being whoever you think Jesus of Nazareth is and understand with me that virtually all of the acts of my Savior Jesus of Nazareth could only represent his initial encounter with a rebellion from this world — his determination, perhaps, when he went out into the desert, where his parole officer couldn't find him, and decided that he had to find the solution within his own heart.

The renegade nature of the saviorship of the mind of Jesus (watch the objection that comes to this!) should be very obvious to you if you'd look at it with me. All of the particulars as a young man, as a growing man anywhere, in his inability to find a relief from what the establishment told him that he had to accept, certainly gave every indication that he spent some of his first years in a form of rowdyism.

Biblically this is very obvious, because when he's first recognized out in the world he is described as a "wine-biber." And they say, "How can this guy, coming out of Nazareth...? And we knew him very well. We also knew the gang that he used to hang out with."

There is always an idea that somehow the lost years of Jesus, that he spent them gaining knowledge in India, where he climbed a peak and questioned a great *mahatma* about what he was. What total nonsense that is! All of the particulars (he's with us here now) represent his determination to find the solution and his inability to do it. Okay?

We were supposed to have a little quiet time here. We started out, beginning to teach the necessity that there's a quiet time and place that you can come to where the resolution has been solved, not in the rowdiness of our determination to find it, certainly in the joy that we felt in our initial encounters not to participate in this world but to formulate a new gang, new ideas where we were going to revolutionize the temple.

That's been true with most of us, and we discovered finally that while the nature of our determination to seek another reality could be fully justified in our decision that there was no solution here, the actual spiritual occurrence of what happened at the time when we suddenly looked at each other and saw that "Hey! This problem cannot be solved." The conversion of the political nature of Jesus in his discovery of the Kingdom of God in the experience that he underwent is virtually identical to the experience that you are undergoing.

So the nature of his revolutionary process, which could be justified in the world and give him a certain authority or power, based on the spoils he was able to gain from the authority, be it in banditry, be it in theft, deserted him as he felt more and more the futility of the revolutionary nature of conceptual mind. It always turned back in on itself.

It's amply demonstrated in scripture when the choice is given to the crowd who should they crucify. Should they crucify this innocent guy standing here, who was telling everybody he's the savior of the world and the Christ and he's using God's power, or should they release Barabbas, who is representing a revolutionary movement in the world that gives them the attraction of their capacity to recognize him? There's no question who the crowd is going to choose. Barabbas was well known as stealing from the rich and giving to the poor. Jesus was well known as only giving to the poor by his determination that being poor in spirit gave the entirety of the resolution. So the choice would be obvious.

Understand this with me. The mind of Jesus is the mind of Barabbas. In fact, the translation is "son of the father." The question is not that. The question is: What father are you the son of? Barabbas is obviously the son of the father of the particulars of the determination to represent yourself in this world. Jesus is obviously the son of our Father in the discovery through the illumination of his mind of the entirety of the solution.

And I've heard all sorts of descriptions of Jesus. Somehow he's a tight-lipped ascetic who walks around in a tight definition of the scripture and demands that you relinquish all ideas of joy and happiness. Not my savior! Do you see that? The other side of a savior is: "He is in rigid conformance with the Old Testament and offers verification of his saviorship within the stricture of the temple." Nonsense! All he really is demonstrating to you at this time is freedom of your own mind, including responsibility for your action (and here's your dilemma in accepting his teaching), an insightful recognition of the nature that the acts that you perform out in the world you will be responsible for, including your revolutionary nature. That's the simple truth of the matter.

So the joy that I am offering you now is the same freedom of overcoming the addiction that Jesus experienced in the desert. When he's confronted by the evil associations, the devil, he says, "I don't want that. Even though I can get the reward of exchange, it's not what I want. I'm going to take the passion in my expression of independence, in my discovery that my independence left me exactly where I was, and I ended up in a conformity with the world."

I began with the idea of the 12-Step Program, the idea of the revolution in the discovery that the problem could not be solved. All around the world we have…. Those who experienced in the Sixties and the Seventies the determination to be independent in the nature of their need to gather as an alternative to the structure have come a long way in the discovery that the solution was actually in their own minds. And they're gathering with us now in this time and place to declare it.

So this first half hour has only got a few minutes left, and what I wanted you to see with me [is] that if I intend to teach you that the solution is within you, I'm going to have to allow you to look at an inventory — are you ready for this? — an inventory of correspondence of what you have done within the entirety of your association. While it's a form of reformation, even unto the recognition of a spiritual awakening, the world is still going to examine you as some sort of perpetrator of acts of variations of the law, and though while you can pay the penalty for it, the world will continue to condemn you and examine you in the nature of their recognition that your recovery occurred only within their concepts without the admission that that's not true.

There's one sentence where this is confirmed in the Gospel of Matthew. It will just take me a minute to read it to you before the break, and then we'll talk about it.

Listen.

Then said he unto them,
Therefore every scribe which is instructed
unto the kingdom of heaven is like unto
a man that is an householder,
which bringeth forth out of his treasure
things new and old.
And it came to pass
that when Jesus had finished these parables,
he departed thence.
And when he was come into his own
country, he taught them in their synagogue,
insomuch that they were astonished,
and said, Whence hath this man
this wisdom, and these mighty works?
Is not this the carpenter's son?
is not his mother called Mary?
and his brethren, James, and Joses,
and Simon, and Judas?
"He has a lot of brothers and sisters."
And his sisters, are they not all with us?
Whence then hath this man all these things?
And they were offended in him.
But Jesus saith unto them,

*A prophet is not without honour, save in
his own country, and in his own house.*

Listen.

*And he did not many mighty works there
because of their unbelief.*

Matthew 13:52-58

Most of you are having that experience now, aren't you? You're undergoing revolutionary realizations of the spirit in the conversion of what formerly was the nature of your need of addiction. Let's use that. And your recovery was entirely spiritual. And you're walking around in the world now in that recovery, carrying an inventory of this world that is very determined not to admit, not to forgive in its entirety the new discovery that has become a part of you. This is occurring all around the world.

What I want you to see with me is that Jesus, our Savior, the Savior of this world, is standing with us in a camaraderie, in a correspondence of friendship, to help us through the hurdle of expressing a spiritual recovery. Can you see that with me? There's no question that you had an insurmountable problem, many addicts, and that your recovery was miraculous, and there's no way that you could have discovered the new happiness and peace that you have found except through the grace of the Holy Spirit, through the grace of turning your will over to God.

So that's the problem. And we're offering the solutions. And we'll talk a little more about it in this next half hour. Remember that God goes with us wherever we go, because God is the Mind with which we think. Okay?

Let's say it together in this recovery idea. All right? We are perfect as we were created. God bless us, every one.

Part II

We're glad you stuck with us here. I know there's perhaps going to be a lot of objection to my description of Jesus. That's okay. He said that if I would serve him, if I would discipline myself to the nature of his recovery, I could discover on my own — this is the addiction program — that through turning my will and my life over to God, which was the entirety of his direction, that I could discover this spiritual recovery and it would make me very happy. And he admonished me further that in that discovery of God I would go out and render service of the recovery that I had made.

This is the entirety of the offering that I am giving to you. The form of repentance in the discovery of a spiritual alternative and my need to express it are the basis of the teaching of Jesus Christ. Removing from him initial human motivations, condemning him to some sort of idol of perfection that came to represent you, is not the nature of my acceptance of him or of what he says to me. He says very simply that "I will represent your recovery from the addiction to death, from the addiction of remaining and finding solace in the representations of momentary relief from pain until you die."

The recovery from the addiction to temporal mind requires the discipline or the necessity to perform continuing acts, first of mind, then on the world, that the alternative is available to you. This is the miracle of the 12-Step Program.

There were some requests. We have a very large network of what we call "recovered 12 Steppers" out in the world that are using the practices both of the Program and of the *Course in Miracles* to express their new discovery. Certainly, recovering from the single problem of the addiction in the recognition of a spiritual awakening can give you, if you continue to pursue it, a realization that the entirety of any problem in this world is within you and that the solution is turning your will over to God. That brings about an illuminate experience of the solution. And I'm speaking from very deep experience.

Obviously, I have a lot of stories to tell in regard to this, including my recovery. And I have told them over a period of a considerable period of years. I probably will continue to tell them.

There's always going to be those who begin to view me as a spiritual healer that are going to inquire, "Did this come about in you in some sort of doctrine that you learned?" and the answer is simply, no. The manner in which I learned this was my inability to deal with the world, and that had nothing to do with how successfully I was able to do it, but simply with the fundamental admission within myself that there was something wrong with this world and the manner in which I viewed it.

Yes, it is a spiritual recovery, and we are enjoying it together, and we do gather and will gather to share the solution.

This is about a three-minute talk on anonymity. What we just expressed to you in the Bible association is a good indication of what you're facing as recovering from your need to be a human being, your determination to express that the power of God has descended on you, and in the miracle you no longer feel the need to represent yourself in fear and attempt to overcome it.

Now, the anonymity of it — and this is from Jesus — is inevitable, very particularly because the expression of it can only actually be shared by those who have had the experience. As objectionable as that may have previously been to you, it's highly true. So we come together with simple realizations and admissions; we couldn't solve the problem. There was a Power greater than our self that could if we would ask Him to, not on our own dependency.

Now, we discover it. We continue to operate in the world, albeit much more successfully (although perhaps not observably so), because we found the peace of God within us. We continued to carry that message out into the world.

We have a book. In case you haven't seen this, there is available to you on the Net, or if you'd like us to send it to you, a little booklet entitled *The 12-Step Program and A Course in Miracles* [See Discourse One]. It's the manner and method by which we have recovered from the addiction of self-will, the idea that "Thy will be done rather than mine."

Is it anonymous? Yes, it is. Yes, it is anonymous. And if we open it up and I'll read from this, I hope you'll send for it. We're using it particularly in our Prison Ministry, because it offers solutions to the young addicts, the revolutionaries who saw very early on that there wasn't any solution here.

All of the acts of violence, many of them that you're seeing around the world now, are acts of war or acts of vengeance, because there doesn't appear to be an enemy that we can vent our rage on. So we begin to vent our rage on each other. And we end up in a confinement because of acts against society.

We want to take these booklets to the young addicts — and we call them "addicts" if eighty percent of them are confined in prisons because of drug-related offenses — so that we can show them that they can change their mind about what they are, not as society defines them, but in a new discovery of themselves. That can mature behind the walls and is maturing, and we're demonstrating it. And we can do it because it's true.

Most of them initially have said, "The world says this and does this. Therefore I won't do what the world tells me to do." This is the incredible dilemma of "Do what I say, not what I do." And that's where the initial rebellion occurs.

So now we've turned that back in on ourselves, and we want to show them that the problem-solving mechanisms employed by the world will no longer satisfy them, that they're going to have to look within themselves for a solution that will be available to them and will broaden their purpose for being here, not that their rebellion against society does not continue, but it becomes a nature of a rebellion that offers an innovating alternative to the condition that was only going to result in death. Can you see this?

So the decision-making mechanism that we offer in the *Course in Miracles* and in the 12-Step Program is one that you can make if your dependence is on God rather than yourself.

Yes. It begins, as you looked at me right there, with some fundamental things like "I'd like to have that be so. I want to have that be so. I wish that that were so. I wish that spiritual healing were so. I can will that it is so, using the Will of God. I can take the power of my mind and express that certainty in what just occurred now in the miracle of the healing procedure."

Is this any different than we would share, having overcome the addiction, where, outside of society for a moment, we continue to express to each other the joy that we feel in the resolution? This is the manner in which my illumination came about. As I progressed in my determination to *serve*, based on the discovery that I had made, my necessity to offer that solution became very intense.

It's a story that most of you have heard. I was very determined that this was a treasure that I could only keep by giving it away. So I began to give it away. I discovered that in the giving of the message of the miracle of my overcoming of the addiction, the joy in giving became more and more intense until, as many of us have done, we take on aspects of only giving in order to keep the joy. This is momentarily, perhaps, a little disruptive in the world. But soon you discover that except in service, you're not happy. Except in giving to the world, you don't find contentment or relief from the pain and tension that will build in you if you are not able to continue to express the innovating discovery of your new mind.

Let's read just a couple of paragraphs from this little book, *The 12-Step Program and A Course in Miracles*. I think you'll find it valuable.

Listen.

*Wherein the necessary process of awakening from
your self-orchestrated dream of pain and death will
be stimulated and accelerated. These are programs of
recovery from an insanely rational, self-perpetuating,
objectively-temporal existence of terminal confinement
that is being misconstrued as some form of the True
Reality that is Eternal Life.*

I wonder who wrote that! So what? It's a good connection. But
it's a recovery from the insanity that you know is this world's
condition. There's a little bit about anonymity here I want to
read you. Why? Those watching this video are beginning to have
experiences of relief from pain. They're being healed. They have
light shining on them. There are spontaneous remissions going
on, and as soon as they go out in the world and declare it, they
are, at a very minimum, asked to "Prove it. Give us evidence of
that," or they're attacked, based on their old references and a
determination not to accept the new man that is emerging.

So what do we do? We end up carrying this message — let's
use Jesus — of his resurrection about with us, holding it
secretly within our heart (and there's a lot of scriptures about
this) because the moment we present it to the world, we
are objectified as some sort of group that found the solution
within the world. And that's not the way it worked, is it?

Listen.

So this is about the importance of anonymity in spiritual
awakening.

*Most Teachers of God in an accelerated spiritual
program of mind/body-enlightenment will discover in
their own intense encounters with a newly-emerging
reality of Christ Mind a highly directive responsibility
for personal anonymity. The more deeply-rooted this
Portico of spiritual rebirth is aligned with Creative
Entirety the more persistent this guardianship will be.*

There's a lot of nice directions in the teachings of Jesus Christ in his New Testament and in his *Course in Miracles* where he says, when the Christ begins to emerge in you, when that discovery comes to you, protect it for a moment. Let it be true and let it emerge. One of his parables says, "Don't let your left hand know what your right hand is doing." Hold onto that discovery and let it grow on its own through practice.

We used to teach this: "Go to meetings." Go to where other ones are studying this *Course*, are beginning to teach it, are representing momentary solutions that they found, even though they couldn't be described out in the world, so that the peace and love, "the pearl worth any price," can be in your heart and mind, can't it?

Let's read a little more.

> *An issuant union with God is sacredly unspeakable and must be protected against the judgmental intrusion of your own corrupt self-constructed identity.*
>
> *Jesus speaks of this repeatedly in New Testament Gospel and in his Course in Miracles as the necessity to guard your own Christ Child and to nurture Its growth through the creative substance of continuing Holy Instants.*

What a lovely idea, that your moment of recovery is going on at this instant and you can nurture yourself on the joy and happiness that we're feeling right now!

Could you recognize that moment of healing? That was a miracle. What did you say to me just a minute ago? "I certainly would like it to be true. I want it to be true. I wish it were true. I think I'll declare it is true. I think I'll declare that in the universe there is a Power, an authority of love through for-giveness, that can show me what I have been searching for out in the world, that I can discover and maintain a momentary relief from all of the pain and loneliness and death that many of us have held, within my own mind, rather than letting the world know the desperation that I actually was feeling.

This is rather a personal video to you, and it's particularly attractive to those who have been sedating yourself in anything, certainly in alcohol and drugs, simply because you couldn't stand this place. I don't know how you could stand it. One of the inquiries that Jesus makes throughout his *Course in Miracles* and New Testament is "How can you stand this slaughterhouse?" You never possessed the normalcy of the human condition. There was always something different about you. And the difference caused more pain rather than less because it was a fundamental requirement from your mind of "What's the reason for this? What's the purpose in it?"

The rebellion that's going on with the young ones now has been simply the inability of their elders, including the original revolutionaries, to find any real purpose for them being here. So emerging now in the transformation of the mind can be a whole new decision that affords immediately an alternative not contained within the reference. And for that moment it will be secret because the expression of it in concepts reduces it to a concept.

"Let go and let God. He will if I let Him. Utilize. Don't analyze." These are all lovely expressions that I have shared for a very long time with those who make initially, perhaps, the discovery through discipline, listening to their elders, listening to those that said to them, "This is a spiritual experience. Stay with it. Practice each day." This is the Workbook, isn't it? Practice each day recognition of the solution of that Holy Instant that's available to you.

Let's complete this:

> *The early founders of the AA Program recognized with profound spiritual insight the importance of the term "anonymous." Certainly in the "confidence" of mutually-confessed "worldly unmanageability." But*

also in the recognition that a personal revelatory experience of the healing power of God may only be expressed through carrying a visionary message of gratitude and freedom to those still imprisoned in the inescapable cycle of drug dependency. In this sense, everyone who discovers the reality of the 'True Love of Creation" is anonymous to this world.

So it is rather anonymous, isn't it? Shall we look at it together just for a moment? And I'll show you the joy that I experience in being able to teach this to you.

The certainty that I am expressing concerning the solution that I found in myself I am offering to you with the certainty that at this time and place we can share it. It's a meeting of our minds, not in the idea of solving a problem in the world where we can share the idea of separation, but meeting together in the certainty that we *have* solved the problem. This is the entire message of Jesus.

We *have* solved this problem. Let's have just one more quiet time today now in the recognition of it, because I want you to be able to take this message with you out into the world.

Listen.

LESSON 326

I Am Forever An Effect Of God

Father, I was created in Your Mind, a holy Thought that never left Its home. I am forever Your Effect, and You forever and forever are my Cause. As You created me I have remained. Where You established me I still abide. And all Your attributes abide in me, because it is Your Will to have a Son so like his Cause that Cause and Its Effect are indistinguishable. Let me know that I am an Effect of God, and so I have the power to create like You. And as it is in Heaven, so on earth. Your plan I follow here, and at the end I know that You will gather Your effects into the tranquil Heaven of Your Love, where earth will vanish, and all separate thoughts unite in glory as the Son of God.

Let us today behold earth disappear, at first transformed, and then, forgiven, fade entirely into God's holy Will.

So that's a prayer, isn't it, expressing the end of this interlude? But it's a prayer of the possibility of a direct contact, a spiritual solution that is so well described in the 12-Step Program, isn't it? It sounds very much like the 11th and the 12th step. Perhaps we'll talk more about it later. But our necessity to maintain a conscious contact with God, asking only to know His Will for us and the power to carry it out, is what we are being offered. And that power now has become, through this prayer of surrender, part of what we are.

We begin to recognize each other, don't we, in the spiritual solutions that we have found, and it makes us very happy to continue to, perhaps, have the anonymity of it, but to recognize that we have found in our sharing a solution that's given us a new direction in this space and in this time.

You're a miracle. I'm a miracle. I know I am, and I know that you know that you are. We are recovering from a terminal disease. We have been born again in that realization. So we can say together — what? — that God goes with us wherever we go because God is the Mind with which we think.

Let's say it together: God bless us, every one.

Welcome Home

Part III

So we're glad you stayed with us in the idea we're going to have a closed meeting. Many of you now are familiar with the 12-Step Program. We have closed meetings and open meetings, and we're inviting the whole world to a closed meeting. It's the recognition that we can come together anywhere in space/time, make immediate admissions to the entirety of our inventory, our inability to solve the problem, our realization that in a mind training we can't choose the curriculum. We're going to have to let all of our faults and all of our indiscretions and everything that occurred with us be laid on the line and begin to practice this program.

And this is the 12-Step Program. And the connection between the *Course in Miracles*, between the mind of Jesus, even to the idea that Jesus suffered from an addiction of joy and happiness that he attempted to find, working in Nazareth, is a true statement. And he progressed very rapidly, based on his determination and the simple founding of the necessity for a solution that you just discovered in your heart and mind.

What does he say about this? He says, "You take this message of love and forgiveness that I am offering you, you work the steps" — let's stay with it just for a minute — "you work the steps of this program because they're going to admonish you that the requirement for discipline is there." All right?

Many of us, when we began to practice the Program and, indeed, the *Course in Miracles* program, were told, "The first thing you do when you get up in the morning is sit down, open the Twenty-Four Hour Book — perhaps you're familiar with Hazelden — and read the prayer for today." For many of us, the idea that we would take *any* amount of time to actually pray or meditate was absolutely not within the nature of the manner in which we were operating in the world. And that certainly included me.

The activity of continually finding and discovering solutions within our own mind in the commerce of the activity of our personal success caused us to build tensions in which we sedated our self. The discovery that we could no longer perform that act and manage our own affairs allowed us at any single moment to look within ourselves and find the solution. This is the direct teaching of Jesus Christ. This is his direct message to you.

The objection of the spiritual seekers in the Program to the religiosity of the stricture of the Christian church or any church would be very obvious to you, because the manner of their solution came from a change of their mind. That is and will be directed by the Christ Mind within them through their willingness to become defenseless in the certainty that they couldn't solve the problem.

Would you like to have it be true that in the new findings of your heart and mind you can actually begin to perform acts of healing, those of you on the Program? What do you think that you've been doing in carrying the message? Everywhere that you have gone as recovered addicts, you have answered the call to offer to those still suffering the solution that you have found. Is that what you have been doing? The connections between the mind training and the Program are so obvious that they're not really open to discussion.

Were you asked on this Program to do a personal inventory of yourself? Were you asked actually to write down the things, perhaps, that you were not particularly proud of that had occurred within your relationship? Of course you were. The entire nature of this offering is to continue to take the inventory and when you're wrong, promptly admit it.

Whew! I got up to Number 10 without even meaning to. *Having had a spiritual awakening as a result of these steps, we tried to carry this program to other addicts and to practice these principles in all our affairs* is the teachings of my Savior Jesus Christ.

My concern about the doctrine of churches, my concern about the political situations of determinations of right and wrong, where they may be true in the concepts, cannot concern me. My concern is to offer the peace and love that I found within my own heart and mind in regard to the healing procedure of the offering of forgiveness.

Let's listen. Let's try just one meditation, should we? These were attempts to be a couple of hours in how we direct the 12-Step Program to the connection of the message of Christ in the New Testament.

Let's listen together.

LESSON 346

Today The Peace Of God Envelops Me,
And I Forget All Things Except His Love.

Father, I wake today with miracles correcting my perception of all things. And so begins the day I share with You as I will share eternity, for time has stepped aside today. I do not seek the things of time, and so I will not look upon them. What I seek today transcends all laws of time and things perceived in time. I would forget all things except Your Love. I would abide in You, and know no laws except Your law of love. And I would find the peace which You created for Your Son, forgetting all the foolish toys I made as I behold Your glory and my own.

And I would find the peace which You created for Your Son, forgetting all the foolish toys I make as I behold Your glory and my own.

And when the evening comes today, we will remember nothing but the peace of God. For we will learn today what peace is ours, when we forget all things except God's Love.

How very lovely to understand how very fundamental the idea of "a day at a time" is in this teaching. *All* happiness and peace of mind is found here and now if it's going to be found, and it can be found only in this time and in this place. This is the discovery that we have made together, isn't it? And this day, well-lived, will suffice. And as it suffices, it will offer us a supply of love and understanding that will transcend the nature of our former grievances.

We have been presenting on these videos the certainty of the power of love and forgiveness to heal physical diseases. Remember, we talked about arthritis and — see? — how the relief came to you at that moment, those that were suffering. This through the power of the Mind of Jesus and the Holy Spirit. See how we talked about Parkinson's? See how we talked about tumors, sicknesses, even unto death, how all kinds can be recovered by a moment of re-centering in this world?

Many of us who have come to this solution based on a recovery from fear or incidences of fear, perhaps, would like to hear what I'm going to say to you now. Everyone watching this video, and most inclusively you, are living somewhere deep within you, in moments of fear. Fundamentally they say, "I am unable to solve this problem." Yet the procedure by which you resolve it allows you to momentarily overcome the panic of the simple reality that you don't know who you are or why you're here or where you came from. And indeed, that is a condition of fear. So you end up projecting it from you and then attacking the world or your brother or yourself, as if somehow the solution to your fear can be found within the relationship that expressed the fear itself.

I want to talk to you for a minute on this. Shall we practice a little bit the relief, how the healing process works? I'm offering spiritual healing to you now, regardless of the problem you have. All of your expressions of fear are simply the denial of the availability of the Love of God through our Sonship, through the Sonship of Jesus, which we now recognize.

In a particular sense, what are you afraid of? To be well. What are you going to lose? All of that grievance that you've been holding on to. If you've made a step with me in overcoming the addiction to the drug and have found a certain relief in a new-found faculty of power of your mind not to act unreasonably or irrationally in the world, both because of the inevitable consequence and also because you have discovered an alternative in which you don't have to perform it, to the direct extent that your awakening process is based on the entirety of your acceptance that you could not solve the problem will be the relief that we can express in sharing that solution with each other. Do you see that with me?

So the process of miraculous healing does not involve addressing the fear in your determination to overcome it, but simply letting the fear come in for a moment to the process of the conversion of your mind in the realization that any rejection that you perform in order to protect your space location can only increase your fear.

The very nature of your bodily function here on earth is to protect your body. Isn't it? Every thing that offends or assaults you in this world requires your protection in order to exist in it. It's an eye-for-an-eye situation. It's the evolutionary process of the survival of the fittest. And as long as you believe you're a Bible — "that you're a Bible"?! [I meant "body"] — that you're a body, the body being the Bible of the resistance to the Love of God, you *will* believe that you are some sort of fleshy animal, still in some sort of evolutionary observation of yourself. The simple fact of the matter is, while that can be a part of your procedure, the solution that you will find is not obtained in surviving, as being fit to stay separate from God, even though your Old Testament may proclaim that to be the solution.

The only solution that will ever show you the entirety of your invulnerability will be laying down the defenses of yourself. All right? Your enemy that appears to be out there, that requires your forgiveness, is only you. You are being attacked by your own thoughts.

"I will not attack myself today. I've decided to let go and let God. I'm going to let the procedures of this program, my realization of a continuing alternative, take over now. Jesus? Holy Spirit? Power greater than myself? I can't do this. Help me. I can't. I'm suffering from a terminal disease. I don't know what to do. I'm in fear. I don't have any answers. I don't want to admit this, but I'm walking around in desperation."

I know you are. That's the human condition. You just can't cover it anymore. I see you out there — and I've got a great deal of experience at this — covering up the desolation that you're actually feeling within your heart. I know every one of you. I have spent many, many generations in helping you, wherever you may be in your procedure, make an admission of the unsolvability of the problem. I've shared with you in the anonymity of your vulnerability my certainty that the truth of you, the certainty of you, cannot be expressed in the commercial association of this world but only in an admission of the entirety of the fear and uncertainty that is deep within you that must be looked at in a moment of the realization of the overcoming of it.

You, there, whoever you may be as a human, any front that you put up with me means absolutely nothing. I did not get this by the doctrine of thumping on the Bible. I did not get this by declaring, "Jesus is my Savior, and you better believe it or you're condemned to eternal hell." That's not the way it worked with me.

I got this for allowing myself to look at the impossible situation contained within my own inventory, asking for relief of it, attempting to make amends to the world that I knew that I had caused pain, recognizing that in my own forgiveness I could feel the joy of the solution.

How many humans, addicts, have I listened to, who have found the solution based on turning their wills over to God? How many have I helped? How many have I attempted to serve to the best of my ability? Thousands. This is what I do. The healing procedure that I discovered came from service in my own discovery.

You want to practice a couple little sentences there, former addicts or continuing addicts?

Say to me, "You've got to give it away to keep it." I'm waiting... It's impossible for you to know that you have found the solution unless you give it away. In the *act* of giving it away — this from our Savior Jesus — you can realize that you're only giving to yourself. Now the joy that you feel is that you're surrounded by a solution. This begins initially with sharing an aggregation, the spiritual solution that you found, by your inability to deal with the problem.

Virtually all of you are familiar with the 12-Step Program, I'm sure. This is what we're taking to the prison ministries. And certainly this is what is out in the world for everyone to look at. The problem with your recognition of the program is fundamentally a denial of the uncompromising nature of it — *un-com-pro-mising* nature of it. That is to say, there's no real alternative to your solution of addiction to death except turning your will and your life over to God. This remains a fundamental admission that the problem was not solvable. You are in a condition where you recognize it momentarily and then continue to solve it.

The uncompromising nature of the teachings of my Savior Jesus Christ showed me that as long as I participated in the world in any illusion of space/time, I could not enter the Kingdom, but that, at any single instant, available to me within this cycle of space/time was the entirety of the solution. So it began with the application of a discipline, of a meditation that expressed the certainty of a need that was not contained within the literature of my human correspondence.

Say to me, "I needed it." Yes. So what do we have? "I wish it were true." "I want it to be true." "I hope it will be true." "It is true."

The expression "It is true" is a discovery of the need for it and your inability to find it, a transformation of your mind now that's giving you a great deal of joy and happiness.

Let's look together just for another moment here now about that place of peace that you have found. We've come together now in an aggregation where somewhere out there we have found the solution and we need to express it. All right? That's perfectly proper. Let's talk about how it came about. But remember this: *How* it came about is not where the solution lay.

You can describe to me all you want about the pain and loneliness and death of this world. I'm very much aware of the ordeal that you went through. I want to show you that that ordeal is a part of the manner in which you can discover a new manner of searching, a new road that's available to you that heretofore was covered by fear.

What the 12-Step Program allows you to do very emphatically is to continue to examine yourself, having determined that you no longer want to do the things that you did because you don't want the consequences of it and you know that if you remain addicted to the drug, you will get the consequences. So we have both that the cause is the drug and the consequences of pain and loneliness or jail time will be there. So it starts out with "I don't want to do this anymore."

The admission that you have one single problem (and in this case we'll use the addictive nature of whatever it is you're taking) formulates the solution, because if that *is* your singular problem — and I assure you, if you believe you're an addict, that you are — the solution will simply be "I'm not going to do that anymore." Your need for help in not doing it is the program of recovery based on spiritual realization.

It's a very fundamental admission that "I can't solve it," but it holds in it all of the solution because it remains intense in its declaration that you have one problem and one solution. In the case of *A Course in Miracles*, the case of the teachings of Jesus, it's: "I have a problem with my own self-will. Everything I do is setting terms for my determination to remain and justify the revenge motivations of this world, and I simply can't handle it anymore. Help me."

Now, the request for help, with the certainty that the problem in the nature in which you attempted to solve it didn't work, will enhance the value of your spiritual realization. We have often seen this expressed as "a moment of desolation." A "bottom," some of us have called it. In the Christian tradition, "a dark night of the soul." And all of us here in this time and place have had these experiences.

The question is not that. The question is whether you recovered from that moment of desolation and are still using the faculties of your own mind in the belief that the solution can be found on this road. The simple truth of the matter is that it can't be. What I want to do with you now, since my attention has been given to you in your discovery of the relief and your determination to carry the message out to the world, is to show you that in that momentary revelation the miracle of your recovery is actually the miracle of the entirety of your recovery from the idea of loneliness and death.

There. Did you see that? That Holy Instant, that moment of here and now, is being expressed by now. See? This is the overcoming of fear. This is the carrying of you, a program that is affording you a continuing solution. You made a decision to turn your will and your life over to the care of God. What an amazing idea, that it was a decision! See? Now, the power of that decision is what we're sharing here together in our discovery of happiness.

We're going to leave you. These are done for television in thirty-minute segments. I hope you'll stay with us or tune in again, and we'll talk a little more about this closed meeting that you've come into where we're going to respect your anonymity in the determination that we share a spiritual discovery.

Remember that God goes with us wherever we go, because God is the Mind with which we think and are operating now in the realization of our own acts of forgiveness.

Let's say it together. God bless us, every one.

Part IV

We're laughing together. We're back with you now, and we're laughing together at how the solution — you'll have to listen to me just for a moment — the solution that we're offering you, the spiritual solution, that man cannot know of the entirety of who he is in the aspects of the idea that he's separate from reality…. That is, very simply, one who is separate cannot know the whole truth because in his separation the whole truth is lost. The basic teaching of this message is one of singularity. You will either be whole and perfect as you were created or you will be separate, which is what nothingness is, since you cannot not be a whole part of Universal Reality.

Now, the message of that certainty can be expressed in a lot of different ways — and is expressed. What I wanted you to see with me in this little 12-Step book and *A Course in Miracles* is that the conceptual observation of it is very simple. Not so simple is the *act* that you are being offered in the discovery of the solution within your own mind. And therein is where the miracle lies.

Yes. Yes. Look how simple this could be for you. In your acknowledgment of this program of recovery — and there are millions of you — I've met you over a period of many years now, and I understand that your recovery has been spiritual. I understand that somewhere you've been unable to express it, and perhaps it's even been reduced to the idea, "You're just going to have to live out the function that you believe that this world has given you." And it's not true.

Your recovery from the ordeal of the conflict that you felt within your own mind was indeed a miracle. The fundamental admission is that "I had nothing whatsoever to do with it." And in *that* admission you will find the joy of sharing communication, unambiguous in its nature because it does not contain judgment.

All of the conflict that you felt or may be still feeling within your idea of the necessity to sedate yourself is based on very rapid necessities for judgment of the existence of your association in this time. The relief that you're experiencing now is simply a determination that you won't judge.

How is the world going to feel about this? It wasn't necessary that you go out and preach to the world, "I'm not going to judge anymore," based on that scripture. The necessity not to judge was based on your solution that no matter how much judging you did, you were never gratified by the idea.

I've heard it said and it's been said for many, many generations that addiction is hereditary. Certainly the idea that you can't deal with the world because of the nature of your creative capacity, your need to justify yourself in relationship with the world, will often lead you to a despondency, simply because you can't express the creativity and joy that you're feeling.

This solution, which is spiritual, spreads your parameter of thought form, and suddenly you begin to teach from your heart. You use your mind, but the joy and the happiness come from your heart and include your participation in this world.

Now, the solution that you have found in that miracle is your certainty that the problems of this world cannot be solved. All right?

We're going to share together here now just a couple of more ideas about the joy that you're going to begin to express, based on God-dependency: "I'm going to depend on God for my solution, not on myself." There was the experience of it. Okay? The light and love of God surrounds you now and gives you a peace of mind that you never thought you could find. And we're sharing it together. Isn't that amazing!

Listen.

> *The roads this world can offer seem to be quite large in number, but the time must come when everyone begins to see how like they are to one another.*

Men have died on seeing this, because they saw no way except the pathways offered by the world. And learning they led nowhere, lost their hope. And yet this was the time they could have learned their greatest lesson.

Listen.

All must reach this point, and go beyond it.

And how many meetings have we been to together, recovered addicts, where the story of desolation, of coming to that point and deciding that the problem could not be solved, how many contemplated suicides, how many ideas of seeking revenge that you just held there and intended to demonstrate in the retention of your own unhappiness? This is a description of what the human condition is, and it's an admission that at that point the solution will be found.

Listen.

It seems to you the world will utterly abandon you if you but raise your eyes.

Yet all that will occur is you will leave the world forever. This is the re-establishment of your will. Look upon it, open-eyed, and you will nevermore believe that you are at the mercy of things beyond you, forces you cannot control, and thoughts that come to you against your will. It is your will now to look on this.

No mad desire, no trivial impulse to forget again, no stab of fear nor the cold sweat of seeming death can stand against your will. For what attracts you from beyond the veil is also deep within you, unseparated from it and completely one.

There is a demonstration of the desolation that you feel. I'm reminded, very much it reminded me — and this is over a period of many years — of where I responded to desperation calls. A lot of you are curious about how I came to my illumination.

One of the factors that I'm disclosing to you now is the manner in which I came to it. This goes back a considerable number of years, but I had a very successful operation in the Western suburbs of a major city, and having discovered the solution in the miraculous recovery from my own addiction, I always felt a strong need to carry the message.

We have, as you are familiar, answering services, where we respond to calls of desperation, or at least calls that indicate they might want to listen to the solution. I had a great need in me to carry the message. If the phone call came, I would go. So it gave me the opportunity to look at you in the nature of your despondency and represent to you what I would hope you would recognize as the solution.

I was surprised. I was examining it this morning. I thought when I might give this talk that you might like to see the nature of my determination that I would go anywhere and do anything to help those in need. As I look back at it, I would get a call and go into a particular part of Chicago where no one, after ten o'clock at night, would even consider going. It didn't occur to me that if I got a call — and it could come from anywhere (you don't know what that situation was going to be) — that I did not respond to it.

In all of those episodes, in all of those times, I was never threatened in any way. There was something about my determination to help that subtracted the idea of fear from my mind. I'm not at all certain that I would do it today, and that belabors it. The fact is that I could go into a situation and say, "Who called?" or "Where is he?" and if I wasn't recognized as a cop (perhaps I might have been recognized as the cop), it could be seen that I had some sort of authority, based on the determination in my mind to perform the act, and no way was it connected to fear.

So the evolvement of the discovery of my need to carry the message had no regard to where I was going to go to do it. This allowed me to end up opening up rehab centers where no one would allow them. That's really going back some years.

I was determined to aid and assist, and in that involvement I began to have these experiences of joy. So the message that I offer and continued in a process of physiological and mental and emotional conversion to the point where my service became first, a mandate of spiritual discovery and then, a realization of the entirety, where a Voice from Heaven said to me, "This is My beloved Son, in Whom I am well pleased."

There's a lot of phenomena going out in the world based on these videos and the healing process, and if you have a story to tell us about this, we'd like to hear from you. This is at the Healing Center. There's thousands of them now. And every one of them is miraculous. And certainly, what just occurred right there, fearful mind, in a decision that you could make, based on my love, while it might not have appeared to you as physical, certainly appeared to you as a fearful episode within your own mind that you've been carrying with you and didn't even know it.

The rebounding from the fear that you had prevented you from actually looking at the magnitude of the fear. Now you're letting that enemy, letting that resistance that you had set up to protect the parameters of your need for that disease, be dissolved in the sharing of our love. And they are dissolved, and we have come together now, in this time, through service to each other. Our Master Jesus says, "Greater things will you do than I have done, because I have prepared a way for you. As you do to the least of me, you do to me." The parable of the Samaritan: "I will help you. I will bind your wounds. I will feed you. And I will harbor you."

So the inquiry as to how I got this, I got it in missionary. There's nothing new about this. All discoverers of the grace of Jesus Christ in any real sense become missionaries. And many of you have opened missions where you afford sustenance of light and love. And the joy that you feel in the necessity to do that is the offering that I am giving you now in the sharing of our love.

So we have come to this time and place, and we were at the point of desolation. And we have recovered from it.

Let's listen just a little more to the message of this 12-Step book and *A Course in Miracles.*

Talk about a day at a time! How about a minute or a second at a time?

Listen.

> *Each day, and every minute in each day, and every instant that each minute holds, you but relive the single instant when the time of terror took the place of love. And so you die each day to live again, until you cross the gap between the past and present, which is not a gap at all. Such is each life; a seeming interval from birth to death and on to life again, a repetition of an instant gone by long ago that cannot be relived. And all of time is but the mad belief that what is over is still here and now.*

Listen.

> *Forgive the past and let it go, for it is gone. You stand no longer on the ground that lies between the worlds. You have gone on, and reached the world that lies at Heaven's gate. There is no hindrance to the Will of God, nor any need that you repeat again a journey that was over long ago.*

What was that offering? Live each moment at a time. Die each second into the certainty of your rebirth. Forgive those who are apparently around you and see that at this time and place the solution is available to you. Listen.

> *Not one light in Heaven but goes with you. Not one Ray that shines forever in the Mind of God but shines on you. Heaven is joined with you in your advance*

to Heaven. When such great lights have joined with you to give the little spark of your desire the power of God Himself, can you remain in darkness?

Seek for that door and find it. But before you try to open it, remind yourself no one can fail who seeks to reach the truth. And it is this request you make today... Put out your hand, and see how easily the door swings open with your one intent to go beyond it. Angels light the way, so that all darkness vanishes, and you are standing in a light so bright and clear that you can understand all things you see. A tiny moment of surprise, perhaps, will make you pause before you realize the world you see before you in the light reflects the truth you knew, and did not quite forget in wandering away in dreams.

What an experience! What an experience! Suddenly the light that was always around you has penetrated your need to defend yourself and attack yourself. What you discovered is your need to addict yourself, to find remedy in drug and alcohol, was simply the manner in which you sustained the pain, because you sought relief outside of yourself. The spiritual relief, the joy of the relief that you have found now in this time and place, can never be lost. This is the light of God that you're carrying around with you now at this time.

Look, your dues have been paid. If you're watching this video with me, there's no necessity that you go back out into that world and continue to perform all the acts that you thought were necessary to sustain yourself, including getting even, including seeking revenge. It's only going to cause you to fall more back into your fear mode and your inability to solve the problem.

So the light is all around you now because you found the solution, and you're willing to stand here just for a moment and enjoy it in its entirety. You have been successful in your program of recovery. Listen.

You cannot fail today. There walks with you the Spirit Heaven sent you, that you might approach this door some day, and through His aid slip effortlessly past it, to the light. Today that day has come. Today God keeps His ancient promise to His holy Son, as does His Son remember his to Him. This is a day of gladness, for we come to the appointed time and place where you will find the goal of all your searching here, and all the seeking of the world, which end together as you pass beyond the door.

This is a day of gladness, for we come to the appointed time and place where you will find the goal of all your searching here, and all the seeking of the world, which end together as we pass beyond the door.

Share with me — and I'm certain that you're doing it at this time — that watching this video of recovery was not by accident. You finally came to a time and place where, having resolved the problem, you were carrying the solution around with you, looking for a new space-light factor that could offer you ideas that would continue to enhance the bright discovery within your own mind.

Yes, you are recovered, and you have come to that place, and it is a miracle. And it is a miracle that can be continued and expanded and extended through forgiveness and love.

Will you please look at this poster with me, that compares the 12-Step Program with *A Course in Miracles?*

I Am Responsible

I am responsible...

I must give it away to keep it.

When anyone, anywhere, reaches out for help, I want the hand of AA always to be there. And for that: I am responsible.

I Am Responsible

When I am healed I am not healed alone. I would share my healing with the world, that sickness and death be banished from the mind of God's one Son, Who is my only Self.

I walk with God in perfect holiness. I light the world. I light my mind and all the minds which God created one with me.

I am responsible, and I am sharing the joy of my acceptance of that responsibility with you. My need to carry this message is extremely intense, and it comes at the direction of my Savior Jesus Christ. He has represented to me the certainty that I discovered in turning my will and my life over to God. By continuing in the practice, he now walks with me in that certainty.

The Christhood of Jesus walks with you as well, because in his solution of forgiveness and love is everything that you have been searching for. And you found it at this time and place.

Yes, we see the light now revealed to us, and we feel just for a moment the joy of the sharing of this program of recovery from death that has given us the surety that our home is in Heaven. And we stay here now just for one more moment to express to each other that light and love as we are healed in the entirety of that dedication.

Father, thank You for the light that we feel descending on us now.

Let's say it together. God goes with us wherever we go because God is the Mind with which we are thinking. Okay?

What a program! What a solution!

Let's say it together. God bless us, every one.

Welcome Home.

All About
A Course In Miracles

To many of you now in this accelerated program of awakening, the continuing observation that not a single human being on earth really knows what it is, where it is, where it came from, or where it is going and nothing at all about itself in relationship to the universe that is apparently all around it, is becoming more and more intolerable.

———————

As a transformative imperative, *A Course in Miracles* will perfectly assist and accelerate the necessary confrontation of your objective self-identify and the whole subjective universe that surrounds you, so that you may undergo your inevitable experience of resurrection and enlightenment.

What you are afraid of, and deny through your own possessive fear, is your own illumination; your returning to God-mind or the memory of your transverse from temporal being to the reality of eternal life. So, it is your transition from death to life, from your old meaningless self-existence that is, in reality, long over and gone. It is a teaching of initiation or the determination of an individual mind to come to its own whole Universal Self.

It is the rite of your passage from time to eternity, from the apparent occurrence of separation to the remembrance that you are perfect as God created you. It is accomplished through a bright reassociation of your individual perceptual self-identity. It is an awakening. This unearthly catechism is directing you to the confrontation of the necessity of parting the veil. Every obstacle that peace must flow across is surmounted in the exact same way. The fear that raised it yields to the love beyond, and so the fear is gone.

Discourses with

The Master Teacher of *A Course In Miracles*:

OTHER BOOKS IN PRINT

———◆◆◆◆———

These are anthologies of transcripts of profoundly transformative talks given through the revelatory mind of the Master Teacher of *A Course In Miracles*. They are ideas about the means and method of the recognition of the transformation of our minds and bodies, as we freely escape together far beyond the boundless Universe that is all about us.

Master Teacher's discourses always ignite intensely emotional responses in participants as they begin to undergo their individual mental reassociation and transfiguration. You may have highly charged enthusiastic responses to this wholly dedicated, totally simple, lovingly communicated message of truth. Indeed, this outpouring of freedom-to-create that occurs through the release of your former necessity to retain self-inflicted loneliness, pain, aging and death, is the bright contagion of whole mind.

These talks will act as a catalyst for you, the reader, in your own self identity of space/time, to undergo the experience of enlightenment necessary to fulfill your inevitable purpose for living: to remember you are whole and perfect as God created you.

The following titles are currently in print:

ILLUMINATION • HOW SIMPLE THE SOLUTION • THE PARADOX OF ETERNAL LIFE • TIMELESS VOICE OF RESURRECTED MIND • GETHSEMANE TO GALILEE • INTRODUCING A COURSE IN MIRACLES • THE RETURN OF THE HERETIC • LOVE

———◆◆◆◆———

FOR MORE INFORMATION VISIT: WWW.THEMASTERTEACHER.TV

www.ingramcontent.com/pod-product-compliance
Lightning Source LLC
Chambersburg PA
CBHW072046080426
42733CB00010B/2012